# Poetry By Wayside

# Book One

# Freedoms Star

# By Wayside

Poetry By Wayside
Book One Freedoms Star
By Wayside

ISBN-13: 978-0615471211

ISBN-10: 0615471218

Printed in the United States of America

Made in the USA

Poetry By Wayside
Book One Freedoms Star
By Wayside

# TABLE OF CONTENTS

Poetry By Wayside
Book One Freedoms Star
By Wayside

The photos/images are from the actual poem of which it was transcribed and typed from and are from the original handwritten, antique manuscript which is over 123 years old of the writings by William McFarland whose pen name was Wayside and which were written in the late 1800s.

Some of the writings and pages in the original manuscript are brittle and falling apart and getting hard to read. Thus it is time now for the works to be printed into a book before they may be lost forever.

Remember these poems are all fictional and of the original writer's imagination and are not real.

Poetry By Wayside
Book One Freedoms Star
By Wayside

# WARNING AND DISCLAIMER

# Other Works

# By Author

# Wayside

If interested, there are also other Wayside books which features poems and/or stories originally written long ago by this same writer as the poems in this book, Wayside.  Printing these books I felt was the only possible way that everyone in my family would be able to see these images, hold them in their own hands and read the poetry.

The first book of fictional stories is entitled, "The Glory World And Guiteau" which is a fictionary or imaginary political story full of political intrigue and may give some clues as to what politics was like in the late 1800s and also talks of immortality and Heaven and Hell and the eternities and life hereafter. It is a short, fictional story about the death and story of President Garfield along with the trial of Charles Guiteau, his assassin, along with some other short political, fictional stories also written by Wayside. Also included with the stories by Wayside is a poem. I have included lots and lots of actual images taken right out of the ORIGINAL HANDWRITINGS BY WAYSIDE out of his original old notebook and have included many photos inside. Again, these were not taken by anyone other than his family members. All of these were handed down from his family who protected and saved these originals and thus even the images are from Wayside's family members.

In the back of that book is a political poem about the same topic, politics from the late 1800s, entitled, "The Machine." Again all of those stories and that poem were also written in the late 1800s and kept hidden and preserved for over 123 years. Some of the images from the actual old, original handwritten text of selected pages from several stories are also included in the book, "The Glory World And Guiteau" by Wayside. The book, "The Glory World And Guiteau" are fictionary stories and are about political issues in the late 1800s. Even the poem has images of its original pages of handwriting. If you like American politics, you are bound to like that book.

http://www.gloryworldandguiteau.com

http://www.thegloryworldandguiteau.com

http://www.waysidebooks.com

http://www.waysidestories.com

See other stories from Wayside as well as some other poems from Wayside in the first two books mentioned.

Poetry By Wayside
Book One Freedoms Star
By Wayside

The second book full of fictional short stories originally written by Wayside is entitled, "Silence In Heaven And The Butter-Woman And Other Wayside Stories" and that book has many wonderful and thought-provoking stories or letters full of imagination and interest on various topics ranging from religion, politics, life and death and the hereafter, and American patriotism. This book, "Silence In Heaven And The Butter-Woman And Other Wayside Stories" also has a few poems in the back of the book. There are many images included in that book as well of selected pages from the original, antique manuscript of Wayside. These fictional stories were also written over 123 years ago. The exact dates are unknown. Some of this book has articles of prayers and one is a Prayer to The Stricken South. This article or prayer came from someone that was an eye witness to the Civil War as he was in it. Thus you have here an eye witness account of the Civil War in that article in this book. Some of these stories in our books are reflections of what was going on at the time and reflections of life in the late 1800s. This gives this book great value. Remember, this book contains stories that to the best of my knowledge were never printed in book form. They are not reproductions. They are brand new although they were originally written prior to 1887.

http://www.silenceinheavenandthebutterwoman.com

Another book full of poems entitled, "Poetry By Wayside, Book Two, Wayside Poetry And Quotations," authored by Wayside which contains many poems about various communities, states and cities and old home life. This book gives some clues as to what life was like in the mid or late 1800s. Although the poems may not be a factual account of the events they do reflect some of the attitudes and the occurrences of the day.

In the back of "Poetry By Wayside, Book Two, Wayside Poetry And Quotations," are also some Proverbs and Quotations which were kept with the same writings and written also by my ancestor, William McFarland, also known as Wayside. Some are Christian or of religious topics and some are of current events, home life and activities going on in his lifetime. Since he lived in the USA in the mid and late 1800s this should be great for history buffs.

The book, "Poetry By Wayside, Book Three, Buds of Promise" authored by Wayside contains even yet more poetry and still more scanned images from his original writings which I myself have personally done using the actual ORIGINAL WRITINGS which were originally written over 123 years ago by Wayside. The Buds of Promise poems in this book, "Poetry By Wayside, Book Three, Buds of Promise" by Wayside here have a lot of spiritual topics of religion and the life eternal and death and dying and gives great hope. Christians should really enjoy that book as well as anyone who appreciates history.

The book, "Poetry By Wayside, Book Four, The Withered Rose, Wayside Poetry, also has a lot of poetry by Wayside along with a great deal of scanned images of handwritten text from its original manuscript by Wayside.

The poems in "The Withered Rose" or Book Four of "Poetry By Wayside" authored by Wayside are full of deep emotions and feelings the writer had in his soul. They are reflections of what was going on at the time and reflections of his life. In "Poetry By Wayside, Book Four, The Withered Rose" there are poems about middle age, getting older, life and death and life eternal.

These books contain words which were written by a Poet of the North and they may have been written in several different states and different years as some of these writings look older than others. Wayside lived in a different time period than what life is like for us now and so the words he wrote and the way he said it is different and yet some of it is still the same. Perhaps some of his writings will give us clues as to how life was back then in the mid and late 1800s which could be very valuable for history buffs. The content of what he was writing does reflect the attitudes and the occurrences of the day, although the poems may not be a factual account.

Poetry By Wayside
Book One Freedoms Star
By Wayside

These poems should be of great interest to someone who enjoys the Civil War history since they were all written by a POET OF THE NORTH. This poet was William McFarland, a/k/a Wayside, and he lived in Indiana, Kansas and Illinois. To the best of my personal knowledge from what my family had told me, none of these poems were ever in a printed book at least not by the family of William McFarland.

I have personally scanned many poems from the original, old brittle pages some of which are torn or ripped of which these very poems were all written and typed from. These scanned images will allow the reader to view his elegant handwriting and view the actual handwriting from the late 1800s which these poems were taken from.

I am using his pen name and continuing on with the family tradition of the pen name of Wayside. Thus ALL of these books that came from his actual poetry AND short stories or articles will have the author's name as the pen name of Wayside.

As the current owner of the original works written by Wayside, I am personally making these scanned images available to other family members to look at so they can view their own ancestor's handwriting. This is all a part of my family's legacy and this is all a part of the family heirloom. I have simply edited where it was extremely necessary and I have sorted, arranged and tried my best to arrange the various poems in topics for the readers to enjoy. This gives to me more value to the family genealogists and historians.

Wayside wrote so many poems and fictional stories that they had to be edited, sorted and placed into several books to be published. Many of the poems in this book are patriotic. Some of the poems in this book, "Poetry By Wayside, Book One, Freedoms Star", are about soldiers in wars and obviously since this author WAYSIDE was in the United States Civil War as a Sergeant, it is very clear to me that some of these poems were written about the Civil War in the USA.

The poem "Yellow Jack" in this book, "Poetry By Wayside, Book One, is very interesting and educational as Yellow Jack was an infection that had a great impact on the Mexican-American war where many suffered from this awful sickness during that war and many soldiers died in that war from the sickness itself.

Wayside paints a picture for you so to speak of his reflections on what was going on at the time and reflections of his life. The content of what he was writing does reflect the attitudes and the occurrences of the day although the poems may not be a factual account. These poems could give the reader a feeling of what it was like to be in the Civil War and what it was like after the Civil War for a Civil War soldier.

For more information or details later see my websites at:

http://www.waysidebooks.com
http://www.waysidestories.com
http://www.waysideletters.com
http://www.waysidepoetry.com
http://www.poetrybywayside.com
http://www.waysidepoems.com
http://www.waysidespoetryworld.com

Poetry By Wayside
Book One Freedoms Star
By Wayside

# DEDICATION

This book is dedicated to my family who has shown and given me much patience and encouragement to finish publishing this book.

This book is dedicated to my cousins because it is also because of them and their need to get their own copy of their family's heirloom that I had decided to make these books and have them available to the public. It is because of my cousin's need to have the photographs of their own ancestor's handwriting that I had decided originally to make as many photos (images which I have scanned using a scanner as well as some photography using a digital camera) and have included them in each book authored by Wayside. I feel the need that the next generations of my family will want and appreciate their own copy of these poems. This was the only way I felt that I could possibly get these images and poems to any of the cousins and their children and their children's children that would want them. Typing, scanning, printing and publishing these books of poetry I felt by doing this if any of the poems are ever lost all my loved ones would have to do would be to order another book which should always be easily available to them. This way the Poetry By Wayside as well as the stories of Wayside will continue.

Poetry By Wayside
Book One Freedoms Star
By Wayside

# ABOUT THE ORIGINAL AUTHOR

William McFarland was a writer and a school teacher from the mid and late 1800s. His pen name was Wayside so that is why I have Wayside along with his name listed as he was the one that wrote these words and he was the one that was the original writer of these Wayside fictional stories, articles, quotations and poems. I arranged, typed and have printed and published these stories, quotations and poems in what I feel would be the way that my ancestor would have wanted under his own name and pen name in printed books. As far as I know none of these were ever printed into a book at least I know they were not by the family of William McFarland since I had the originals and since those before me had them kept hidden practically under a rock. I have taken his writings that he had in an old notebook and separated some of them, sorted them and arranged them in a way that they could be typed onto a home, personal computer and then added the scanned images of selected text from the original writings which these poems were typed directly from the originals. Remember all of these images were taken directly from the old, brittle and sometimes torn paper where these poems were written and thus some of it was not in good condition. After all, they are only 123 or more years old.

Poetry By Wayside
Book One Freedoms Star
By Wayside

William McFarland was a real person that lived from 1823 to 1887. He was born on 29 Dec. 1823 in Bucklestown, Berkeley County, West Virginia. He died on 12 Sept. 1887. He lived in Virginia, Indiana, Kansas and Illinois. He was a teacher in several states. His family also lived on a farm as his parents owned a farm. His father, John McFarland, was a shoemaker by trade as well as was that of his grandparents and great grandparents. His mother's name was Elizabeth Bailey. William McFarland's grandfather was William McFarland who was in some of the Indian Wars and was a British soldier. His grandmother was a Nancy Kilgore whose family were shoemakers.

William McFarland (Wayside) was also a Union officer in the Civil War for the United States of America. Thus he is one of my Civil War ancestors. He was a poet of the North. To find so many wonderful, thought-provoking and educational poems and short stories written in this time period is quite unique.

The original writer, William McFarland, was married to Anna Virginia Donaldson, who was my great, great, great grandmother and they had five daughters. One of these daughters, Elizabeth Adelaide McFarland, was my great, great grandmother and she was married to a Milton Edison Wicks who was my great, great grandpa. They had a daughter named Minnie Elizabeth Wicks, who was my great grandmother. Minnie Elizabeth Wicks was married to Franklyn Rockwell Wilson. They had two daughters and a son.

The information and the photos or scanned images that are in this book are not, to my personal knowledge and best abilities, easily accessible anywhere else.

The images (photos) inside this book and any on the cover of this book as well as the other books mentioned above were taken from the actual old, original handwriting of Wayside from his actual, original manuscript which is over 123 years old. Anyone that appreciates and enjoys old handwriting or anything old for that matter should enjoy looking at the images in these books. Some of these original pages are brittle and thus it is time to preserve them by typing them up and putting them into book form for the future generations and for the general public at large. The originals many of which are not in good condition and are yellowed, are written by a quill pen and some of it is in pencil. Such elegant, beautiful handwriting that I know many will appreciate seeing the scanned images which we have included of the original manuscript pages which these poems were written on and saved for over 100 years on fine-quality paper.

The thoughts and feelings are from Wayside and not from me. Remember these words were written in the late 1800s.

It was the goal and desire of Wayside that his writings would be published into a book but he did not live long enough to achieve his goal and so I am doing this for him.

Poetry By Wayside
Book One Freedoms Star
By Wayside

William McFarland was my great, great, great grandpa
on my father's side. I was doing my family genealogy
and found out that this particular ancestor was once
upon a time a writer and a school teacher and had
written poetry. Since then I had the desire to find
these poems. Fortunately for me I located the distant
relative that had owned these poems and short stories
and he gave them to me as he wanted a younger
family member to have them and he could tell how
much they meant to me and how much I enjoyed
them.

With the age of the internet and with home
computers, scanning devices and with digital cameras
it is now time that the works be printed and published
for anyone to read that wishes to.

May my family and their descendents preserve,
protect, cherish and hand down from one generation
to another generation their own personal copies of
Wayside's poems in a form that they can obtain now
themselves. This way it will be fair to everyone in the
family that they can have something special handed
down as a family heirloom from at least one of their
ancestors.

Since it has now been 150 years after the start of the
Civil War, which was the very war this original author
of these poems was in and fought for, I feel it is
extremely important to get these words out to the
general public this year as this year marks the 150th
Anniversary of the start of the Civil War.

These words of poetry were NEVER published in a book form except through me on behalf of my late ancestor, William McFarland. Some of these poems' images may have with them another poem that is not inside this book. I have copied them the way they were on the page using a scanner and some of the poems also had another poem or several poems on the same page. Thus, those poems if not in this book would be in another one of my books of "Poetry By Wayside."

Please also remember that there are several other poems that are also in my other book now published and it is currently easily available, "Silence In Heaven And The Butter-Woman And Other Wayside Stories." Some fictional stories, articles and even some prayers of general themes, religion and patriotic in nature are in that printed book. Some are about the Civil War such as the prayer, "Prayer for the Stricken South." This book would be one for history buffs that are looking for articles about the Civil War.

There is also a poem entitled, "The Machine" which is all about American politics and Garfield and Guiteau, the Republicans and the Democrats and the original poem was also written in the late 1800s by Wayside and is now in my published book, "The Glory World And Guiteau." Said book is also now printed and is published and is currently available online.

Poetry By Wayside
Book One Freedoms Star
By Wayside

There were simply so many poems I had to make decisions on where to put what poem and there were too many to put in a single, paperback book so there had to be several paperback, printed books made available.

All of these poems and the photos and scanned images contained in all of these printed books have been copyrighted.

# Poetry By Wayside

# Book One

# Freedoms Star

# By Wayside

Poetry By Wayside
Book One Freedoms Star
By Wayside

# A Gem

The verdant plains of Neponset,
Made rich with labor, toil, and sweat,
Made richer still by men of worth,
Excell'd by none upon this earth.
Neponset's daughters wake the strain,
With music fill this prairie plain,
And let those matchless songs arise
In loud Hosanna's to the skies.

                            Wayside

## Billy and Orene

8

When troubles dark did o'er me roll,
When untold sorrows filled the soul,
A gentle word, a bright warm [?]
A welcome smile upon you Orene.

9

When ready to sink in deep despair,
When darkness filled both earth and air,
The hand of God did intervene,
And sent me Billy and Orene.

10

Can I forget those dearest friends,
Who always true did me befriend?
When crushed and bleeding and in need,
Found in them both true friends indeed?

11

Let sun and moon refuse to shine;
Let palsy chill this tongue of mine;
Let reason fail & I forget,
My two best friends in [Oquawset].

*Requete*

## A Gem

The verdant plains of [Oquawset],
Made rich with labor, toil, and sweat,
Made richer still by men of worth,
Excelled by none upon this earth.
[Oquawset's] daughters wake the strain,
With music fill this prairie plain,
And let these matchless songs arise
In loud Hosannahs to the skies

# A Little Gem

A little gem has passed away;
A floweret sweet of yesterday;
A little rosebud closed its eyes,
To ope anew in Paradise.
Its precious dust doth lowly lay
And mingle with its kindred clay;
A mother's hand hath mark'd the spot
A symbol, flower, forget-me-not.

                                    Wayside

## My Old Friend

concluded
to J. C. Peters

My dearest friends Oh, where are they!
Gone to other lands away;
Can I forget them? Never will;
On mem'ry's page they're living still.

The thoughts of friends of former years
Start up aflush my hopes and fears,
A keen desire, a constant strain;
The hope that we shall meet again.

10

But time is passing, short the stay,
Soon from earth we'll pass away;
Faith, hope, and love inspire the strain,
And tells me we shall meet again.

Wayside

## A Little Gem.

A Little Gem has passed away,
A flow'ret sweet of Yesterday;
A Little Rose bud clos'd its eyes,
To ope anew in Paradise.
Its precious dust doth lowly lay,
And mingle with its kindred clay;
A mother's hand hath made the spot
A Symbol, flower, forget-me-not.

Wayside

Buds of Promise
136

Now all the girls with ...
With wit and understanding;
Would like to have him for a Beau;
This man from Swigerts Landing.

137

Tis passing strange how the world moves;
Things hard of understanding;
So handsome Fair one captive led
By one called Swigerts Landing.

138

Then all the Ladies cried aloud
Began to reprimanding;
This gentle maid for what she said
About young Swigerts Landing

Wayside

A Gem

A little gem has pass'd away,
A flower sweet of yesterday;
On wings of light its spirit flies
To bloom anew in Paradise
Its precious dust doth lowly lay,
To mingle with its kindred clay,
A mothers hand doth mark the spot,
A simple flower Forget-me-not.

Wayside

# A Good Name

## LINES TO LIZZIE

### 1.

A name, what is it, can you tell,
Where peace and comfort ever dwell?
Where grace and beauty both combine,
And make the human face Divine?

### 2.

A name so dear and rich and sweet
In all things kind, and loving, neat,
Always cheerful, always busy;
Like my own dear Darling Lizzie.

### 3.

A priceless boon to man on earth,
The greatest good.  The greatest worth;
In Heaven and earth it is the same;
The grandest prize, is a good name.

4.

The next in worth a pleasant face,
Made sweeter still by modest grace;
All aglow with sacred love
Like those of the bright-above.

5.

Kind gentle one, can I forget
A primrose dear in Neponset
Did often meet in mirthful play,
And turned my darkness into day.

6.

Indulgent one think me not rude,
I could not, would not, dare intrude;
This poem I to you confide,
A special tribute from Wayside.

Wayside

# A Good Name

A name, what is it, can you
Where peace and comfort ever d...
Where grace and beauty both c...
And make the human face...

2

A name so rich and sweet
dear and
In all things kind, and lovin...
Always Cheerful— always...

# A Good Name

Lines to Lizzie Miller

1

A name, what is it, can you tell,
Where peace and comfort ever dwell?
Where grace and beauty both combine,
And make the human face Divine?

2

A name so rich and sweet *dear and*
In all things kind, and loving, neat,
Always Cheerful—always busy;
Like my own dear Darling Lizzie.

3

A priceless Boon to man on earth
The greatest good, The greatest worth;
In Heaven and earth it is the same;
The grandest prize is a good name.

4

The next in worth a pleasant face,
Made sweeter still by modest grace;
All aglow with sacred Love
Like those of the Bright-above.

5

Kind gentle One, can I forget
As primrose dear in & Ponset
Did often meet in Mirthful play,
And turned my darkness into day.

6

Indulgent one think me not rude,
I could not, would not, dare intrude;
This Poem I to you Confide,
A special tribute from Wayside.

Wayside

# A Good Time

### 1.

Oh, when you want a good time;
One that's rich and rare;
One that's truly sublime,
Call the ladies there.

### 2.

Call in the Nymph like fairie,
Young, and tender, green.
Call in the bright and airy,
Gay, and sweet sixteen.

### 3.

Then seek the grove so sweet
And through its bowers rove
Where birds do warbling greet
Their mates with song of love.

### 4.

In nature's green, gay bower,
When perfumes fill the air;
Come, while away an hour
In converse with the fair.

5.

When music fills the breeze
While waves the green trees top,
Adoring smile upon your knees,
And then the question pop.

6.

Then Heaven will open to view,
Stars shall brighter shine,
And angels dance above the blue
To hear those words "I'm thine."

7.

Then live and love, let life explain,
Nor sink from coming strife;
But try them well and you will gain
A treasure, and a wife.

## A Good Time

**1**

Oh, when you want a good time;
One that's rich and rare;
One that's truly sublime,
Call the Ladies there.

**2**

Call in the nymph like fairie,
Young, and tender, green.
Call in the bright and airy,
Gay, and sweet sixteen;

**3**

Then seek the grove so sweet
And through its bowers rove
Where birds do warring greet
Their mates with song of love

**4**

The native's green, gay bower,
When perfumes fill the air;
Come, while away an hour
In converse with the Fair.

**5**

When music fills the breeze
While waves the green tree tip;
A daring smile upon your knees,
And then the Question pop.

**6**

Then Heaven will ope to view
Stars shall brighter shine,
And angels dance above the blue
To hear those words "I'm thine,"

**7**

Then live and love, & life explain,
Nor shrink from Coming Strife;

# All Away

### 1.

Oh!  So lonely, all the day!
None to cheer me!  All away!
No strong arm to hold me up;
Alone, must drink life's bitter cup.

### 2.

As time moves on with rapid tread,
I find no place to lay my head;
No beacon-fire, no light in view,
But, all alone my way pursue.

### 3.

All is dark!  All is night!
All are faded!  Gone from sight;
The shrill winds whistle to an fro,
As lonely through the world I go.

### 4.

Still darker grows the lonesome road;
And heavy on my heart a load;
Which weighs me down in double woe;
As lonely through the world I go.

## 5.

All my hopes of life are gone;
Like chaff before the winds are blown;
All pleasure gone -- faded the light,
All is dark and black as night.

## 6.

Nothing is left for me on earth;
For all is gone of any worth;
Nothing for me, but groans and sigh,
Only awhile, and then to die.

## 7.

I look towards the rugged steep
Over-hanging cliff where waters deep;
And there to plunge beneath its roar,
And hide myself forevermore.

## 8.

My home's a blank a desert shore;
And love to me will come no more;
The fire is out and I alone;
And none to comfort!  No, not one.

9.

I feel the life's blood ebbling flow,
My time is short with things below;
The bleak winds sigh and loudly roar,
And howl in triumph evermore.

10.

This burden, toil; this care and strife.
Cause me to mourn and say "What's life"
And what is all this world to me,
When nought is left but misery?

11.

Soon I shall pass away from earth,
And all that's dear, of any worth;
Soon I shall leave all things below;
Leave (And) none to tell where I do go.

# All Away

## 1

Oh! so lonely, all the day!
None to cheer me! all away!
No strong arm to hold me up;
Alone, must drink lifes bitter cup.

## 2

As time moves on with rapid tread,
I find no place to lay my head;
No beacon-fire, no light in view,
But, all alone my way pursue.

## 3

All is dark! All is night!
All are faded! — Gone from sight;
The shrill winds whistle to an fro,
As lonely through the world I go

## 4

Still darker grows the lonesome

The shrill winds whistle to and fro,
As lonely through the world I go

### 4

Still darker grows the lonesome road;
And heavy on my heart a load;
Which weighs me down in double woe;
As lonely through the world I go.

### 5

All my hopes of life are gone;
Like Chaff before the winds are blown
All pleasure gone — faded the light
All is dark and black as night.

### 6

Nothing is left for me on earth;
For all is gone of any worth;
Nothing for me, but groans and sigh,
Only awhile, and then to die.

### 7

I look towards the rugged Steep
Oer-hanging Cliff where waters deep;
And there to plunge beneath its roar,
And hide myself forever more

# All Away

### 1

Oh! so lonely, all the day!
None to Cheer me! all away!
No strong arm to hold me up;
Alone, must drink lifes bitter cup.

### 2

As time moves on with rapid tread,
I find no place to lay my head;
No beacon-fire, no light in view,
But, all alone my way pursue.

### 3

All is dark! All is night!
All are faded — Gone from sight;
The shrill winds whistle to and fro,
As lonely through the world I go

### 4

Still darker grows the lonesome road;
And heavy on my heart a load;
Which weighs me down in double woe;
As lonely through the world I go.

### 5

All my hopes of life are gone;
Like Chaff before the winds are blown;
All pleasure gone — faded the light
All is dark and black as night.

### 6

Nothing is left for me on earth;
For all is gone of any worth;
Nothing for me, but groans and sigh,
Only awhile, and then to die.

### 7

I look towards the rugged Steep
Oer hanging Cliff where waters deep;
And there to plunge beneath its roar,

## All Away

8

My Home's a blank a desert shore;
And Love to me will come no more;
The fire is out and I alone;
And none to comfort! no notice.

9

I feel the Life-blood ebbling flow—
My time is short with things below;
The bleak winds sigh and loudly roar,
And howl in triumph evermore.

10

This burden, toil; this care and strife,
Cause me to mourn and say "What's life"
And what is all this world to me
When nought is left but misery?

11

Soon I shall pass away from earth,
And all that's dear, of any worth;
Soon I shall leave all things below;
Leave (And) none to tell where I do go.

# AWAY BOYS AWAY

## CLOSE OF SCHOOL

### 1.

The school is over, and all play'd out;
We here no longer stay;
But wheeling right and left about,
And march, march away.
The old school house we bid adieu,
And playmates bright and gay;
The world moves on a merry crew;
Away Boys, Away,

> Awa -y- Awa-y!
> For sunshine and the day!
> The school is out and I am free,
> Away Boys Away!!

### 2.

Our slates and pencils, and our books
Will bother us no more.
A merry life for girls and boys
Is standing at the door.
We thank our teachers, one and all;
And bid a kind good day;
No more lessons for us to learn
Away Boys Away!

        Awa-y Awa-y!
        'Tis freedoms happy day!
        No more lessons for us to learn
        Away Boys Away!

### 3.

Our fathers and our mothers, dear!
They always hail the day,
With joy, with gladness and with smiles,
The closing, happy day.
This happy day, the close of school,
O may we ne'er forget
The lively times, the closing scene,
We had in Neponset

        Awa-y Awa-y!
        For sunshine's happy day
        The world moves on a merry crew
        Away Boys Away!

## 4.

This world is full of toil and strife;
And full of pain and woe;
An earnest care give busy life,
As through the world you go.
My little children may you all,
The storms of life outride;
And find a home in Heaven above
Along with old Wayside.

Awa-y Awa-y!!
Above the starry plain,
Where youth immortal ever bloom,
May we all meet again.

Wayside

291

## Away Boys Away

Close of school

The school is over, and all play'd out;
We here no longer Stay;
But wheeling right and left about,
And march, march away.
The old school house we bid adieu
And playmates bright and gay;
The world moves on a merry crew;
Away Boys, Away,
        Awa——y, Awa——y!
        For sunshine and the day!
        The school is out and I am free,
        Away Boys Away!!

Our Slates and pencils, and our Books
Will bother us no more.
A merry life for Girls and Boys
Be standing at the door.
We thank our teachers, one and all,
And bid a kind good day;
No more lessons for us to learn
Away Boys Away!
        Awa——y, Awa——y!
        'Tis freedoms happy day!
        No more lessons for us to learn
        Away Boys Away!

Our Fathers and our Mothers, dear!
They always hail the day
With joy, with gladness and with smiles,
The Closing, happy day.
This happy day, the close of school,
O may we ne'er forget
The lively times, the closing scene
We had in Sconset
        Awa——y, Awa——y.

# April In 1881

## A Long Winter

The sun it shines bright,
The sky it is clear;
But it's chilly and cold,
For its snow every-where.

Young chanticleer crows
While frost fills the air,
Counts eggs by the dozen,
And snow every-where.

The farmers all grumble,
Begin to despair,
Because there is nothing
But snow every-where.

Wayside

## Beautiful Home — Since to Miss Hattie Belle

8

Those handsome girls and Boys at play,
Those beautiful forms so bright and gay,
A beautiful thought doth in me arise,
That beautiful Home for them in the skies.

9

I tell its grand, its good and its neat,
Those beautiful children in school to meet,
The minds brightest thoughts beginning to glow,
Revives the old scenes of long, long ago,

10

A Beautiful Girl I often do meet,
On going to school when crossing the street,
Her name is so handsome quite easy to spell,
This beautiful Girl is Miss Hattie Belle

                              Wayside


April in 1881   A long winter

The sun it shines bright,
The sky, it is clear;
But its chilly and cold,
For its snow everywhere.

Young chanticleer crows
While frost fills the air,
Counts eggs by the Dozen,
And snow every-where.

The farmers all grumble,
Begin to despair,
Because there is nothing
But snow everywhere

# A Sheep's Eye

### 1.

When twilight gray it's mantle spreads,
In social chat bobs many heads,
And sly winks show the one who weds
                    A Sheep's Eye.

### 2.

What thing is this that makes one feel
So very queer?  'Tis loves fair deal --
Unlocks the heart, and breaks the seal,
                    A Sheep's Eye.

### 3.

The boys and girls oft meet and chat,
About this thing, then about that,
Another thing that looks so flat,
                    A Sheep's Eye.

### 4.

I fell in love with a nice young Squire,
Which put my heart and head on fire;
I long'd for something queer desire,
                    A Sheep's Eye.

### 5.

I felt a quiver in every limb,
Was no one there could equal him,
He made my heart and head to swim
              With a Sheep's Eye.

### 6.

What could this be that made me start
That reached way down into my heart,
'Twas loves sweet smile 'twas cupids dart,
              A Sheep's Eye.

### 7.

A subtle snare to catch the bird,
The queerest thing you ever heard
And yet to all the most absurd
              A Sheep's Eye.

### 8.

I passed unto the other side,
To find a nice good place to hide;
'Twas no avail for soon I spied,
              A Sheep's Eye.

## 9.

Then I began to laugh and cry,
I felt so good, could not tell why
Still brighter beam'd that thing, O my!!
                    A Sheep's Eye.

## 10.

This world is full of mirth and fun,
For every maid and mother's son,
And the fellow with that one,
                    A Sheep's Eye.

## 11.

There's nothing in this world so funny,
Make one feel rich without money,
A fountained fill'd with milk and honey,
                    A Sheep's Eye.

## 12.

When in the church, it greets me there,
A nod, a wink and then a stare,
Co fund the thing!  It's everywhere,
                    A Sheep's Eye.

### 13.

And when they all kneel down to pray,
When prayers ascend the Milky-Way,
A peep behind reveals that day
      A Sheep's Eye.

### 14.

When in the doorway he doth stand,
He bewitching and looks bland,
Then casts at me that magic wand,
      A Sheep's Eye.

### 15.

It touch'd my heart, a love-like pain,
When suddenly he wink'd again,
That funny thing, I saw it plain,
      A Sheep's Eye.

### 16.

When sleep creeps over me at night,
In dream-land sometimes take a flight,
And there I see that vision bright,
      A Sheep's Eye.

### 17.

And now young ladies every-where,
Of your honor take good care,
And of this monster all beware.
      A Sheep's Eye

22
Bade farewell to Brandy, Rum, and Gin,
And cut the products of the man of Sin;
Piece a beacon fire bright as the sun;
Which tells me the millennium has begun.

23
Farewell to grog-shops whisky-cards and dice;
And all the mean and petty haunts of vice;
Piece a better home for those we love
On earth a while and then then in Heaven above.

24
Now, Boys of manhood and of honor bright,
Come Join the P.C. & G.T. this night,
Here on this altar swear you'll never be
Found drunk on the streets and disorderly.
                              Waysides By Levi

A Sheeps Eye
                    The P.C. of G.T. Inscription
When twilight gray its mantle spreads,
In social chat bows many heads,
And sly winks show the one who reads
                    A Sheeps Eye.

2
What thing is this that makes one feel
So very queer? Tis loves Zeal that—
Unlocks the heart, and breaks the seal,
                    A Sheeps eye.

3
The Boys and Girls at meet and chat,
About this thing then about that,
Another thing that looks so flat,
                    A Sheeps eye.

## A Sheep's Eye

I fell in love with a nice young squire,
Which put my heart and head on fire,
I long'd for something — Queer desire,
      a Sheep's eye.

I felt a quiver in every limb,
Was no one there could equal him,
He made my heart and head to swim
      with a Sheep's eye.

What could this be that made me start
That reached way down into my heart,
'Twas loves sweet smile 'twas cupits dart,
      a Sheep's eye.

A subtile snare to catch the bird,
The queerest thing you ever heard,
And yet to all the most absurd
      a Sheep's eye.

I pass'd unto the other side,
To find a nice good place to hide;
'Twas no avail for soon I spied,
      a Sheep's eye.

Then I began to laugh and cry,
I felt so gay I could not tell why,
Still brighter beam'd that thing, O my!!
      a Sheep's eye.

This world is full of mirth and fun,
For every maid and mothers son
And the fellow with that one,
      a Sheep's eye.

# A Sheep's Eye

11

There's nothing in this world so funny,
Make one feel rich without money,
A fountain gilt with milk and honey,
        A sheep's eye.

12

When in the church, it greets me there,
A nod, a wink and then a stare,
I found the thing! It's everywhere,
        A sheep's eye.

13

And when they all kneel down to pray,
When prayers ascend the Milky-way,
A peep behind it's that day,
        A sheep's eye.

14

When in the doorway he doth stand,
He twist wing and looks bland,
Then casts at me that magic wand,
        A sheep's eye.

15

It touch'd my heart's love like pain,
Then suddenly he wink'd again,
That funny thing, I saw it plain,
        A sheep's eye.

16

When sleep creeps over me at night,
For dream-land sometimes take a flight,
And there I see that vision bright,
        A sheep's eye.

17

And now young ladies every where,
Of your honor take good care,
And of these monsters all beware,

# A Soldier Of The Cross

### 1.

God's promises to us are given;
A better home for all, in Heaven;
Where souls immortal ever bloom
Beyond the clouds, beyond the tomb.

### 2.

Yes far beyond the upper deep,
Where mortals never wake to weep;
But, bask in light forever more
On Canaan's high and happy shore.

### 3.

Eternal truth of love divine;
From everlasting I am thine;
Thy grace sufficient, doth sustain,
And tells us we shall live again.

Wayside

## A Soldier of the Cross — concluded

God's promises to us are given,
A better Home for all, in Heaven;
Where Souls Immortal ever bloom
Beyond the Clouds, beyond the Tomb.

Yes far beyond the upper deep,
Where mortals never wake to weep;
But bask in light forevermore
On Canaan's High and Happy Shore.

Eternal Truth of Love Divine;
Thine Everlasting Name thine;
Thy Grace sufficient, doth sustain,
And tells us we shall live again.

Wayside

### In Memoriam

The Old Arm chair in vacant spot;
Unoccupied, alone;
While whispered words throughout the night
Proclaims a loved one gone.
O! look above the mystic height,
See visions bright and fair,
Look! Behold! In spotless white,
A living Father there.

Wayside

### Charlie and Willie

My Willie and my Charlie, too!
Have passed away from this low sphere,
To bloom in that pure zone above
Where all is life, and light, and love.
My daughter wipe your weeping eyes,
And with look up above the skies,

# Beautiful Home

### 1.

A beautiful home in Heaven above;
A beautiful home where all is love;
That beautiful home; that pure, bright chime;
That beautiful home in Heaven is mine.

### 2.

This world is beautiful where we live;
This beautiful world which God did give
Abounds in beauty on land and sea;
This beautiful world, God gave to me.

### 3.

Those beautiful stars that shine so bright;
That twinkles beautiful all the night;
The beautiful moon and dazzling sun
Is God's free gift to everyone.

### 4.

In this good world I wish to stay
'Til God in his love shall say "Come Away"
I wish to stay here until I die,
And then go to God in that beautiful sky.

## 5.

Those beautiful worlds that's hung on high,
Is the home of the saints who never die;
A Heavenly home divinely fair;
God and the angels all are there.

## 6.

How dear to my heart my old Native Home;
The valleys and hills, where I used to roam;
Those blossoms and flowers spread over the plains
I long for the pleasure to pluck them again.

## 7.

That sweet little cottage there in the grove;
And beautiful meadows where I did rove;
Where birds do sing in the trees so fine;
That beautiful home in the grove is mine.

## 8.

Those handsome girls and boys at play,
Those beautiful forms so bright and gay;
A beautiful thought doth in me arise,
That beautiful home for them in the skies.

9.

I tell it's grand, it's good and it's sweet;
Those beautiful children in school to meet;
The mind's brightest thoughts beginning to glow;
Revives the old scenes of "Long, long ago."

10.

A beautiful girl I often do meet,
Or going to school when crossing the street;
Her name is so handsome quite easy to spell,
This beautiful girl is Ms. Hattie Belle.

Wayside

## Beautiful Home

Lines to
Miss Hattie B. L.

**1**

A beautiful Home in Heaven above,
A beautiful Home where all is love;
That beautiful Home, that pure, bright clime,
That beautiful Home in Heaven is mine.

**2**

This world is beautiful where where we live;
This beautiful world which God did give
Abounds in beauty on land and sea;
This Beautiful world, God gave to me.

**3**

These beautiful stars that shine so bright,
That twinkle so beautiful all the night;
The beautiful moon and dazzling sun
Is God's free gift to every one.

**4**

~~Nothing I would wish to~~
In this good world I wish to stay
Til God in his love shall say "Come away"
I wish to stay here until I die,
And then go to God in that beautiful sky.

**5**

Those beautiful worlds that's hung on high,
Is the Home of the saints who never die;
A Heavenly Home Divinely Fair;
God and the angels all are there.

**6**

How dear to my heart my old Father Home,
The valleys and hills, where I used to roam;
Those blossoms and flowers spread over the place
I long for the pleasure to pluck them again

**7**

That sweet little cottage there in the grove,
And that beautiful meadow where I did rove
Where birds do sing in the forest so fine,

Beautiful Home          Sweet Miss Hattie Bell

8
Those handsome Girls and Boys at play,
Those beautiful forms so bright and gay
A beautiful thought doth in me arise,
That beautiful Home for them in the skies.

9
I tell its grand, its good and its neat,
Those beautiful children in school to meet
The minds brightest thoughts beginning to glow
Revives the old scenes of long, long ago

10
A Beautiful Girl I often do meet,
On going to school when crossing the street,
Her name is so handsome quite easy to spell,
This beautiful Girl is Miss Hattie Bell

                              Wayside


            April in 1881   A long winter
The sun it shines bright,
The sky it is clear;
But its chilly and cold,
For its snow everywhere.

Young chanticleer crows
While frost fills the air,
Counts eggs by the Dozen,
And snow every-where.

The farmers all grumble,
Begin to despair,
Because there is nothing
But snow every where

# BILLY AND IRENE

### 1.

Kind, gentle muse unfold in rhyme,
With beauty blend each word and line;
Give grace to thought, then grasp the prize
The inspiration of the skies.

### 2.

Quick my good pen the mind obey,
And gather the gems that round me play;
Bid sparkling thoughts new life impart,
Electrify and cheer the heart.

### 3.

Ye wing'ed gods of the upper deep;
With magic touch my pencil steep;
And cause the brightest thoughts to glow
And glisten like the frosted snow.

### 4.

Bid rays of light around me shine;
With choicest fill every line.
Come, lift the veil, dispel the gloom,
With holy incense fill the room.

### 5.

Embellish all prepare the way,
And light the soul to living day,
Bid forms Divine like incense rise,
And scale the grandeur of the skies.

### 6.

Just like a dream we float away,
A bubble on the morning spray;
Unnotic'd, unknown soon we fall,
And then oblivion covers all.

### 7.

Thus mortal man that's born below,
Like prairie flowers come and go;
Their wither'd forms around me lie
And tells me man is born to die.

### 8.

When troubles dark did o'er me roll,
When untold sorrows fill'd the soul;
A gentle word, a light was seen,
A welcome smile from you Irene.

## 9.

When ready to sink in deep despair,
When darkness filled both earth and air;
The hand of God did intervene,
And sent me Billy and Irene.

## 10.

Can I forget those dearest friends,
Who always true did me defend?
When crush'd and bleeding and in need,
Found in them both true friends indeed?

## 11.

Let sun and moon refuse to shine;
Let palsy chill this tongue of mine;
Let reason fail if I forget,
My two best friends in Neponset.

Wayside

## Billy and Irene

1
Kind, gentle muse unfold in rhyme,
With beauty blend each word and line;
Give grace to thought, then grasp the prize
The inspiration of the skies.

2
Quick my good pen the mind obey,
And gather the gems that round me play;
Bid sparkling thoughts new life impart,
Electrify and cheer the heart.

3
Ye winged gods of the upper deep;
With magic touch my pencil sweep;
And cause the brightest thoughts to glow
And glisten like the frosted snow.

4
Bid rays of light around me shine;
With choicest fill every line.
Come, lift the veil—dispel the gloom,
With beauty's presence fill the room.

5
Embellish all the — prepare the way
And light the soul to living day;
Bid forms divine like incense rise
And steal the grandeur of the skies.

6
Just like a dream we float away,
A bubble on the morning spray;
Unnoticed, unknown soon we fall,
And then Oblivion covers all.

7
Thus mortal man that's born below,
Like prairie flowers come and go;
Their —

## Billy and Crane

When troubles dark did o'er me roll,
When untold sorrows filled the soul,
A gentle word, a light was lent,
A welcome smile from you Crane.

When ready to sink in deep despair,
When darkness filled both earth and air,
The hand of God did intervene,
And sent me Billy and Crane.

Can I forget these dearest friends,
Who always have did me defend?
When crushed and bleeding and in need,
I found in them both true friends indeed?

Let sun and moon refuse to shine;
Let palsy chill this tongue of mine;
Let reason fail if I forget
My two best friends in Deponset.

*Wagrile*

## A Gone

The verdant plains of Deponset,
Made rich with labor, toil, and sweat,
Made richer still by men of worth,
Excelled by none upon this earth.
Deponsets daughters wake the strain,
With music fill this prairie plain,
And let these matchless songs arise
In loud Hosannahs to the skies

# COMMENCEMENT

### 1.

Behold the Light!  Its lustre sheds,
A halo o'er a sea of heads.
Those Buds of Promise, happy free,
Rocked in the cradle of Liberty.

### 2.

The germs of thought that ope to view;
That sparkle like the morning dew;
Engages in sweet coming strife;
To bad and blossom into life.

### 3.

Behold the anxious, earnest, gaze;
Of Fathers, mothers - loving face;
We see it all - the glad surprise
In tears of joy that fill their eyes.

### 4.

The dawn of life's work is begun;
We see it in the rising sun;
We see it in the blooming fair,
The light of progress every-where.

## 5.

Pervades all space; it fills the room;
Makes Heaven and Earth and Nature bloom;
It cheers the heart, doth it refine;
And makes the face almost divine.

## 6.

O, let me mount and soar away,
And mingle with the morning spray,
To carry the news to life's bright sun,
The Millennium has begun.

## 7.

The world of progress moves in light,
And scales the steep untrodden height;
Unbosoms thought, expands in love,
And rises to the Bright-Above.

## 8.

We here behold those children dear,
Whose minds reach towards a higher sphere,
A grander plain on which to find,
A Heaven below for all mankind.

9.

Travel this world all to an fro,
And search the depths far down below;
Find nothing than can raise our joys,
Like progress in our girls and boys.

10.

A father's hope, a mother's joy,
Is that advancing bright-eyed boy.
A pledge from Heaven born of love,
To live on earth, and then above.

11.

A daughter fair, the sweetest prize,
Brings incense down from sunny skies;
Spell-bound we view the fine array,
Of culture, tase, in that essay.

12.

Friends and neighbors all have come,
And crowd in ev'ry niche of room;
To see, and hear, whatever bright,
To sparkle from those lips to night.

## 13.

This night is hallow'd it is blest,
The Star of Progress, brightest, best;
In mansions great, or, humble cot,
This scene will never be forgot.

## 14.

But live and smile through life's bright day,
'Til loves sweet dream has pass'd away,
'Til faith is lost in loves desire,
'Til God shall say "Come up higher."

## 15.

The dearest place to me on earth,
My old school-house and native hearth;
And those dear girls and boys at play,
Where we spent life's summer-day.

## 16.

O'er forty years have pass'd away,
Since last I saw that circle gay;
But oft in vision sweetly gleam,
Their photos in the land of dream.

## 17.

I see them still, I see them plain!
The girls and boys at play again!
They form a ring; it's just the same!
Play "Drown the Duck" the same old game.

Poetry By Wayside
Book One Freedoms Star
By Wayside


### 18.

There's others skipping gaily round;
Hearts full of glee, over they bound;
O, my, what music, what a roar,
As round the school-house they do pour.

### 19.

There, one fell down and bumped his nose,
Another one he stump'd his toes;
Then each began a plaintive call,
To roar as loud as they could ball.

### 20.

Again I see them in the house,
All quit; still as any mouse;
Afraid to speak, or stir, in school,
Of that big switch, or, teacher's rule.

### 21.

That switch it laid there plain in sight,
Which did both boys and girls affright;
I would surely trounce each girl and boy,
If any should the school annoy.

### 22.

But Progress brought about a change;
Gave freedom-thought, a wider range;
Denounc'd the switch and ferule-rule;
Made better laws to govern school.

## 23.

The whip, the scourge was laid aside;
Then love, not fear it did preside;
And wiser grew the men that day,
When they threw the stick away.

## 24.

Appeal was made to manly pride,
When they laid the stick aside;
The Star of Hope shone brighter when,
They said ladies little men.

## 25.

The world grows brighter ev'ry day;
When wisdom rules and love bears sway;
I see a vision bright as the sun!
The Millennium has begun!

Wayside

# Commencement

### 1

Behold the Light! Its lustre sheds
A halo o'er a sea of heads.
Those Buds of Promise, happy free,
Rocked in the Cradle of Liberty.

### 2

The germs of thought that ope to view,
That sparkle like the morning Dew;
Engages in sweet coming strife;
To bud and blossom into life.

### 3

Behold the anxious, earnest, ~~earne~~
Of Fathers, Mothers— loving face;
We see it all— the glad surprise
In tears of joy that fill their eyes.

### 4

The dawn of Life's work is begun;
We see it in the rising sun;

# Commencement

**8**

We here behold those Children dear,
Where minds reach toward a higher,
A grander plain on which to find
A Heaven below for all mankind.

**9**

Travel this world all to an fro,
And search the depths far down below
Find nothing than can raise our
Like progress in our Girls and Boy

**10**

A Fathers Hope. A mothers joy,
Is that advancing Bright-eyed Boy.
A pledge from Heaven & born of love,
To live on earth, and then above.

**11**

And nothing than can raise us up
Like progress in our Girls and Boys.

10
A Fathers Hope, A Mothers joy,
Is that entrancing Bright eyed Boy;
A pledge from Heav'n Their of love,
To live on earth, and then above.

11
A daughter fair, The sweetest prize
Brings incense down from sunny skies
Spell bound we view the fine array
Of Culture, taste, — in that essay.

12
Friends and neighbors all have come
And crowd in ev'ry niche of room
To see, and hear, whatever bright,
To sparkle from those lips to night.

13
This night is Hallow'd it is blest,
The Star of Progress, brightest, best;
In mansions great, or, humble Cot,
This scene will never be forgot.

14
But live and smile through lifes brig
Til loves sweet dream has past
Till faith is lost in loves desire

15

Thee dearest place to me on earth—
My Old School House and native hearth;
And those dear Girls and Boys at Play,
Where we spent lifes Summer day.

16

O'er Forty years have passed away,
Since last I saw that circle gay;
But oft in vision sweetly gleam,
Their Photos in the land of Dream.

17

I see them still, I see them plain!
The Girls and Boys at play again!
They form a ring; its just the same!
Play "Drown the Duck," the same old ga

18

There's others skipping gaily roun
Hearts full of Glee, 'ror they boun
O my what music, what a roar

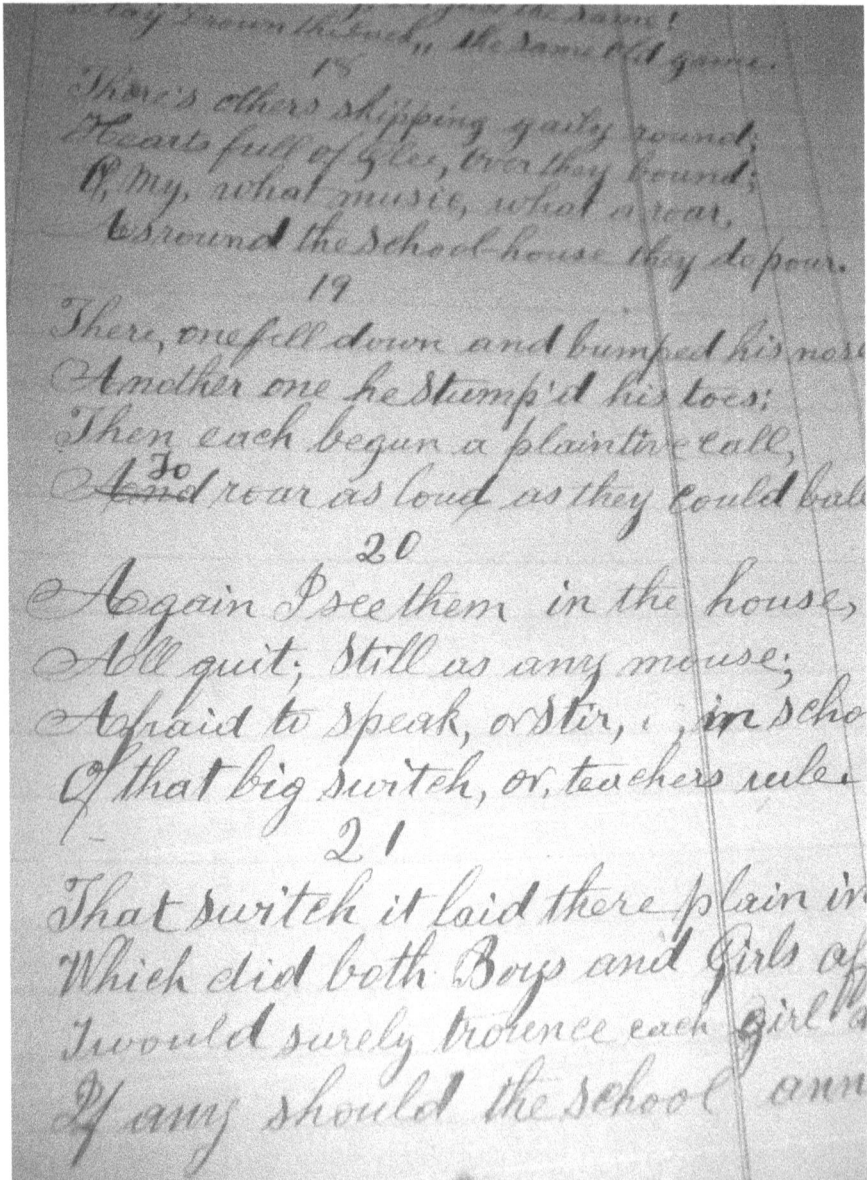

18

There's others skipping gaily round,
Hearts full of glee, over they bound;
O, my, what music, what a roar,
Around the School house they do pour.

19

There, one fell down and bumped his nose,
Another one he stump'd his toes;
Then each began a plaintive call,
And roar as loud as they could bawl

20

Again I see them in the house,
All quit; still as any mouse;
Afraid to speak, or stir, in scho
Of that big switch, or, teachers rule

21

That switch it laid there plain in
Which did both Boys and Girls of
I would surely trounce each girl
If any should the school ann

Commencement                    Concluded

22

But Progress brought about a change
Gave Freedom thought, a wider range
Denounced the switch and harsh rules;
Made better laws to govern schools.

23

The whip, the scourge was laid aside;
Then Love, not fear it did preside;
And wiser grew the men that day,
When they threw the stick away.

24

Appeal was made to manly pride
When they laid the stick aside;
The Star of Hope shone brighter when
They said Ladies Little men.

25

The world grows brighter every day;
When wisdom rules and love bears sway;
I see a vision bright as the sun!
The Millennium has begun!

229

## Commencement

1

Behold the Light! Its lustre sheds
A halo o'er a sea of heads.
These Buds of Promise, happy, free,
Rocked in the Cradle of Liberty.

2

The germs of thought that ope to view;
That sparkle like the morning dew;
Engages in sweet coming strife;
To bud and blossom into life.

3

Behold the anxious, earnest ~~earnest~~ gaze;
Of Fathers, mothers — loving face;
We see it all — the glad surprise
In tears of joy that fill their eyes.

4

The dawn of Lifes work is begun;
We see it in the rising sun;
We see it in the Blooming Fair,
The light of progress every where.

5

Pervades all space; it fills the room;
Makes Heaven and Earth and Nature bloom;
It cheers the heart, doth it refine;
And makes the face almost Divine.

6

O, let me mount and soar away,
And mingle with the morning spray;
To carry the news to lifes bright sun
The Millennium has begun.

7

The world of Progress moves in light,
And scales the steep untrodden hight;
Unbosoms thought, expands in love;

## Commencement

**8**

We here behold those Children dear,
Whose minds reach tow'ard a higher sphere,
A grander plain on which to find
A Heaven below for all mankind.

**9**

Travel this world all to an free,
And search the depths far down below;
Find nothing than can raise our joys
Like progress in our Girls and Boys.

**10**

A Fathers hope, A Mothers joy,
Is that advancing Bright-eyed Boy;
A pledge from Heaven & born of love,
To live on earth, and then above.

**11**

A daughter fair, The sweetest prize
Brings incense down from sunny skies;
Spell-bound we view the fine array
Of Culture, taste, in that essay.

**12**

Friends and neighbors all have come
And crowd in ev'ry niche of room;
To see, and hear, whatever bright,
To sparkle from those lips to night.

**13**

This night is Hallow'd it is blest,
The Star of Progress, brightest, best;
In mansions great, or, humble Cot,
This scene will never be forgot.

**14**

But live and smile through lifes bright day,
Til loves sweet dream has passed away
Till faith is lost in loves desire

233

## Commencement  *Continued*

15

Thee dearest place to me on earth—
My Old School-House and native hearth;
Amid those dear Girls and Boys at Play,
Where we spent lifes summer-day.

16

O'er Forty years have pass'd away,
Since last I saw that circle gay;
But oft in vision sweetly gleam,
Their Photos in the land of Dream.

17

I see them still. I see them plain!
The Girls and Boys at play again!
They form a ring; its just the same!
Play "Drown the Duck," the same old game.

18

There's others skipping gaily round;
Hearts full of Glee, O'er they bound;
O, my, what music, what a roar,
As round the school-house they do pour.

19

There, one fell down and bumped his nose,
Another one he stump'd his toes;
Then each began a plaintive call,
And roar as loud as they could bawl.

20

Again I see them in the house,
All quit; still as any mouse;
Afraid to speak, or stir, in school
Of that big switch, or teachers rule.

21

That switch it laid there plain in sight,
Which did both Boys and Girls affright;
I would surely trounce each Girl and Boy

Commencement       Concluded

### 22

But Progress brought about a change,
Gave Freedom—Thought, a wider range;
Denounc'd the switch and Ferule rule;
Made better laws to govern school.

### 23

The whip, the scourge was laid aside;
Then Love, not fear it did preside;
And wiser grew the men that day,
When they threw the stick away.

### 24

Appeal was made to manly pride
When they laid the stick aside;
The Star of Hope shone brighter when
They said Ladies Little men.

### 25

The world grows brighter every day;
When wisdom rules and love bears sway;
I see a vision bright as the sun!
The Millennium has begun!

# Dash Away Boys

### 1.

The school is out shouts everyone,
Nothing to bother; now for fun;
Come girls and boys, all, let us run,
   Dash-away Boys, Hurrah!
   Hurrah Boys Hurrah!
   Dash-away Boys, Hurrah's Cheer!

### 2.

We laugh and giggle, and whisper in school;
And often break the teacher's rule,
But never tell we're cheek by jale
   Dash-away Boys, Hurrah!
   Hurrah Boys, Hurrah!
   Dash-away Boys Hurrah, Cheer!

### 3.

We're sometimes naughty, cut a swell;
Yet love our teacher passing well;
And that's the truth.  Now boys pell, mell!
   Dash away Boys, Hurrah!
   Hurrah Boys, Hurrah!
   Dash-away, Boys Hurrah!  Cheer!!!

4.

Our teacher's good, yes, very dear!
In concert let us give her cheer;
And tell her come another year,
   Dash-away Boys, Hurrah!
   Hurrah!  Boys Hurrah!
   Dash away Boys Hurrah!!  Cheer!

5.

We sometimes lose our equipoise;
And then we make a deal of noise
That's nought for us, we're girls and boys
   Dash away Boys, Hurrah!
   Hurrah Boys Hurrah!
   Dash-away Boys Hurrah, Cheer!

6.

As summers day doth smoothly glide;
At morning, noon, and eventide
We'll sing the song of Old Wayside
   Dash away Boys Hurrah! Cheer!!!

     Wayside

Poetry By Wayside
Book One Freedoms Star
By Wayside

---

## Dash Away Boys

1. The school is out shouts every one,
   Nothing to bother; now for fun;
   Come Girls and Boys, all, let us run,
       Dash-away Boys, Hurraw!
       Hurrah Boys Hurraw!
       Dash-away Boys, Hurraw; Cheer!

2. We laugh and giggle, and whisper in school;
   And often break the teacher's rule,
   But never till we're cheek by jole
       Dash-away Boys! Hurraw!
       Hurrah Boys, Hurrah!
       Dash-away Boys Hurraw, Cheer!

3. We're sometimes naughty, cut a swell;
   Yet love our teacher passing well;
   And that's the truth. Now Boys Pell mell,
       Dash-away Boys, Hurraw!
       Hurrah Boys, Hurrah!
       Dash-away Boy Hurraw! Cheer!!!

4. Our teacher's good, yes, very dear!
   In concert let us give her Cheer;
   And tell her come another year,
       Dash-away Boys, Hurrah!
       Hurrah! Boys Hurrah!
       Dash away Boys Hurraw!! Cheer!

5. We sometimes lose our equipoise;
   And then we make a deal of noise
   That's nought for us, we're Girls and Boys
       Dash-away Boys Hurraw!
       Hurraw Boys Hurraw,
       Dash-away Boys Hurraw, Cheer!

6. As summer's day doth smoothly glide;
   At morning, noon, and eventide

# EDWARDS APPEAL

### 1.

Untold troubles round me roll,
That blights the prospect of the soul;
They weigh me down in double woe,
As, lonely through the world I go.

### 2.

My hopes are gone!  A buried whole!
Yea, out of sight -- beyond control.
No light to shine upon my way,
To gilds life's close, eventful day.

### 3.

The early bliss of days gone by,
In blasted heaps around me lie;
In gratitude has done her part,
And pierc'd again the bleeding heart.

### 4.

With all my hopes and prospects blasted,
And all the misery I've tasted;
Can loves sweet dream to me impart,
A balm for this, my broken heart?

5.

God's blessings round unnumber'd roll,
Which sooths and warms the dying soul;
But thoughts of former days loom up,
And fill with pain life's bitter cup.

6.

My home despoiled, a loved one gone!
No one to hear me make my moan;
There is a void that nought can fill.
Except, it be death's bitter pill.

7.

Mid sorrows deep, with anguish bent,
Must travel the steep descent.
O, cannot love, or, pity thaw,
The frozen heart of a mother-in-law!!

8.

O, bid me live!  Let love make room,
And virtue with your graces bloom;
Bid light to shine remove the flaw;
Restore my Kate!  My mother-in-law.

## 9.

O how can I submission yield;
And leave to fortunes fickle field;
That one so dear to me, and kind;
My own true loving Kate behind?

## 10.

Can I forget my darling mate?
That cherish'd one my loving Kate?
Nothing on earth could from me draw,
My darling, but, a mother-in-law.

## 11.

Cold, chilling winds around me roar;
Which tears agape the bleeding sore;
And dark black clouds obscure the day,
When thinking of my Kate away.

## 12.

Mid life's gay dream we float away;
A bubble on the morning spray;
Unknown, unnotic'd, soon we fall;
And then oblivion covers all.

## 13.

This life is all we have below;
Bitter and sweet where're we go;
More bitter still, O!  Who can draw,
The picture true.  A mother-in-law!

## 14.

A pain, a shadow makes me start;
O'er whelms me with a broken heart;
That one, O dear!  How can I hate
The mother of my darling Kate.

## 15.

That darling one, come life come death;
Yet while I live my latest breath,
Shall lisp the praise of one I love;
Believing we shall meet above.

## 16.

Yea, far beyond the ether blue,
And bask in light like angels do.
Rejoice in that pure zone above;
Where all is life, light and love.

## 17.

But let me live awhile on earth;
In this good land that gave me birth;
Open your heart, the treasure give!!
Then Heaven will bless and I shall live!!

## 18.

Open the door, prepare, make room!
With welcome greet both Bride and Groom!
Give back my Kate and then you'll draw!
All honors due a mother-in-law.

## 19.

But "No" said she there is no room;
"You fooled away a pleasant home;
You're false, untrue, unkind, ingrate!
You forfeited my daughter Kate!!

## 20.

No love nor pity can I trace!
While darker grows that scowling face!!
Her fang-like fingers sharpen'd claws!!
Reveals to me my mother-in-law!

### 21.

Ah!  Luck less fate why me pierce?
Why pierce the heart clean through and through,
Leave nothing but a sadden'd groan!!
A blasted reed to walk alone!!

### 22.

Pray what is this, that robs me quite?
That steals my senses, shuts my sight?
What makes me shudder, groan and?
And almost makes me wish to die?

### 23.

A friend incarnate everywhere,
Doth follow me, and, at me stare.
A hook-ed bill and peak-ed chin,
The very picture of old sin.

### 24.

Doth chill my heart and pains my head;
And makes me wish that I was dead.
I hated, curse'd her very life,
Because she stole away my wife.

### 25.

A long, gaunt leopard, cross and old;
The witch of end or an old scold;
No peace nor comfort could I draw,
From this old crone my mother-in-law.

## 26.

A proud, old granny on the wing;
So very good, would pray and sing.
At church a saint, at home a devil,
And that's the way she holds things level.

## 27.

Her very looks did me affright;
I sometimes dare not sleep at night;
Afraid that she a knife would draw,
And cut my throat, my mother-in-law.

## 28.

Cyclones and storms and hurricanes,
Which sweep across our western plains,
Are nothing in comparison,
For Satan reigns In that old one.

## 29.

See how she strides across the floor,
Mad as the devil to shut the door.
Sucks poison with an old Rye-straw;
And then squirts venom my mother-in-law.

## 30.

There was a time, I did invest,
In loving one, the brightest best;
With heart sincere I aske'd be mine?
She gave a kiss and answer'd "Thine."

### 31.

Ecstatic rapture fill'd my soul;
I lov'd her as a perfect whole;
This love co-equal was return'd;
And ever in my bosom burn'd.

### 32.

Days, weeks, and months did smoothly glide,
For darling Kate was by my side;
My joys were full, did over-flow,
And made a little Heaven below.

### 33.

But why do I those days recall,
While shadows darken like a Pall;
I fell!  I lost my first-estate;
I lost!  I lost, my darling Kate!

### 34.

That vampire, crone, she follow'd me!
And by device and strategy,
Poison'd the ears of my dear mate;
And robbed me of my darling Kate.

### 35.

Let palsy strike her poison tongue,
And at her grave no song be sung;
Bid storms and winds howl ev'ry-where.
Of mothers-in-law all beware.

# Edwards Appeal

1

Untold troubles round me roll
That blights the prospect of the soul;
They weigh me down in double woe,
As, lonely through the world I go.

2

My hopes are gone! As buried whole!
Yea, out of sight—beyond control,
No light to shine upon my way
That gilds lifes close, eventful day.

3

The early bliss of days gone by,
In blasted heaps around me lie;
Ingratitude has done her part
And pierc'd again the Bleeding Hea[rt]

4

With all my hopes and prospects b[?]
And all the misery I've tasted
Can loves sweet dream to m[?]
A balm for this, my broken he[art]

5

And blessings round unnumber[ed]

Edwards Appeal continued
2nd part

Pray what is this, that robs me quite?
That steals my senses, shuts my sight?
What makes me shudder, groan and ?
And almost makes me wish to die?

23
A fiend Incarnate every where
Doth follow me, and, at me stare.
A hook-ed bill and peak-ed chin,
The very picture of Old Sin.

24
Doth chill my heart and pains my head;
And makes me wish that I was dead.
I hated, curs'd her very life,
Because she stole away my wife.

25
A long, gaunt leopard, cross and old;
The Witch of Endor an old scold;
No peace nor comfort could I draw
From this old Crone my mother-in-la

26
A proud old granny on the wing;
So very good would pray and sing.
At church a saint, At home a Devil,
And that's the way she holds things level.

... in my bosom burn'd.

### 32

Days, weeks, and months did smoothly
For Darling Kate was by my side;
My joys were full did ober-flow
And made a Little Heaven below.

### 33

But why do I those days recall
While Shadows darken like a Pa...
I fell! I lost my First-Estate;
I lost! I lost, my darling Kate!

### 34

That Vampyre, Crane, She follow'd
And by device and strategy,
Poison'd the ears of my dear mate
And robbed me of my Darling K...

### 35

Let palsy strike her poison tongu...
And at her grave no song be sun...
Bid Storms and winds howl o...
Of Mothers in Law all bewere...

## Edwards Appeal

**1**

Untold troubles round me roll
That blights the prospect of the soul;
They weigh me down in double woe,
As, lonely through the world I go.

**2**

My hopes are gone! As buried whole!
Yea, out of sight— beyond control,
No light to shine upon my way
To That gilds lifes close, Eventful day.

**3**

The early bliss of days gone by,
In blasted heaps around me lies,
Ingratitude has done her part
And pierc'd again the Bleeding Heart.

**4**

With all my hopes and prospects blasted,
And all the misery Ive tasted,
Can loves sweet dream to me impart,
A balm for this, my broken heart?

**5**

Gods blessings round unnumber'd roll,
Which sooths and warms the dying soul;
But thoughts of former days loom up,
And fill with pain lifes bitter cup.

**6**

My home despoiled, A loved one gone!
No one to hear me make my moan,
There is a Void that nought can fill,
Except, it be deaths bitter pill.

**7**

Mid Sorrows deep, with anguish bent,
Must travel the steep descent.
O, can not love, or, pity thaw

8

O, bid me live! let love make room,
And virtue with your graces bloom;
Bid light to shine remove the flaws;
Restore my Kate! My Mother-in-law.

9

O how can submission yield;
And leave to fortunes fickle field,
That one so dear to me, and kind;
My own true loving Kate behind.?

10.

Can I forget my darling mate,?
That cherish'd one my loving Kate?
Nothing on earth could from me draw
My darling, but, a mother-in-law.

11

Cold, chilling winds around me roar;
Which tears agape the bleeding sore;
And dark black clouds obscure the day;
When thinking of my Kate away.

12

'Mid lifes gay dream we float away;
A bubble on the morning spray;
Unknown, unnotic'd, soon we fall;
And then Oblivion covers all.

13

This life is all we have below;
Bitter and sweet where'ere we go;
More bitter still, O! who can draw
The picture true. a Mother-in-law!

14

A pain, a shadow makes me start;
O'erwhelms me with a broken heart;
That one, O, dear! how can I hate

101

## Edwards Appeal        continued

### 15

That Darling One, come life come death;
Yet while I live my latest breath
Shall lisp the praise of One I love;
Believing we shall meet above.

### 16

Yea, far beyond the ether Blue,
And bask in light like angels do.
Rejoice in that pure Zone above;
Where all is life Light and Love.

### 17

But let me live awhile on earth;
In this godd land that gave me birth;
Open your heart, the treasure give!!
Then Heaven will bless and I shall love!!

### 18

Open the door, prepare, make room, !
With welcome greet both Bride and Groom;!
Give bah my Kate and then you'l draw!
All honors due a Mother-in-law.

### 19

But "No" said she there is no room;
"You fooled away a pleasant home;
You'r false, untrue, unkind, Ingrate!
You forfeited my Daughter Kate !!

### 20

No love nor pity can I trace,!
While darker grows that scowling face!!
Her fang-like fingers sharpen'd claws,!!
Reveals to me my mother-in-law!

### 21

Ach! luckless fate why me purse?
Why pierce the heart clean through and throu;
Leave nothing but a sadden'd groan.!!

22
Pray what is this, that robs me quite?
That steals my senses, shuts my sight?
What makes me shudder, groan and?
And Almost makes me wish to die?

23
A fiend Incarnate every where
Doth follow me and, at me stare.
A hook-ed bill and peak-ed chin,
The very picture of Old Sin.

24
Doth chill my heart and pains my head;
And makes me wish that I was dead.
I hated, cursed her very life,
Because she stole away my wife.

25
A long, gaunt leopard, cross and old;
The Witch of Endor an old scold;
No peace nor comfort could I draw
From this old Crone. My mother-in-law.

26
A proud old granny on the wing;
So very good would pray and sing.
At church a saint, At home a Devil,
And that's the way she holds things level.

27
Her very looks did me affright;
I sometimes dare not sleep at night;
Afraid that she a knife would draw
And cut my throat, My mother-in-law;

28
Cyclones and Storms and Hurricanes,
Which sweep across our western plains,
Are nothing in comparison.

245

## Edward's Appeal  concluded

**29**

See how she strides across the floor,
Mad as the D—l to shut the door.
Sucks poison with an old Rye-straw,
And then squirts venom my mother-in-law.

**30**

There was a time, I did invest,
In loving one, the brightest best;
With heart sincere I asked Be mine?
She gave a kiss and answer'd Thine,,

**31**

Ecstatic rapture fill'd my soul;
As I lov'd her as a perfect whole;
This love co-equal was return'd;
And ever in my bosom burned.

**32**

Days, weeks, and months did smoothly glide,
For Darling Kate was by my side;
My joys were full did over-flow,
And made a little Heaven below.

**33**

But why do I those days recall
While shadows darken like a Pall;
I fell! I lost my First-Estate,
I lost! I lost, my darling Kate!

**34**

That Vampyre, Crone, She follow'd me!
And by device and strategy,
Poison'd the ears of my dear mate,
And robbed me of My Darling Kate,

**35**

Let palsy strike her poison tongue,
And at her grave no song be sung;
Bid storms and winds howl everywhere

# Epha Belle

### 1.

Come gentle muse unfold in rhyme,
And let it answer well;
And make the one to shine sublime;
The modest Epha Belle.

### 2.

A blushing rose-bud-smiles so sweet,
Her name it sounds so well;
With sparkling eyes and looks so neat;
They call her Epha Belle.

### 3.

This modest fair one goes to school,
To learn to read and spell;
And when the teacher calls her out,
She answers Epha Belle.

### 4.

Poetic name; it charms the ear;
Can any grief, or, tell
The full true name of one so fair,
As charming Epha Belle.

5.

Now all the girls that go to school,
I love them passing well;
Obey your teacher, mind the rule,
Keep pace with Epha Belle.

6.

And now dear pupils one and all,
Strive always to excel;
Let nothing keep you out of school,
But, come with Epha Belle.

7.

The girls have all sweet names I know,
But none does this excel;
This handsome name where did you go
To find it Epha Belle?

8.

Miss Gerrand is your teacher good;
Maybe she can tell;
And let all know about the one,
We call Miss Epha Belle.

## 9.

Now all good girls that go to school
Must learn their lessons well;
And each shall a poem like
The one to Epha Belle.

Wayside

273

Tapping on the window — concluded

5

Now I understand the reason
Of this cold and stormy season
Were they not afraid of freezin'
  By living there alone?
Pray advice to all is this
Dear Girls dont be remiss,
  But take the ring and kiss,
    And never sleep alone.

6

Let winds blow high or low
Let winters come and go
Were safe from frost and snow
  Describe it O, who can!
What made this lovely strife?
What makes a merry life?
What was it made a wife?
  Who made the Rib for man?

Wayside

Epha Belle

1

Come gentle muse unfold in rhyme,
  And let it answer well;
And make the one to shine sublime
  The modest Epha Belle.

2

A blushing rose-bud smiles so sweet,
  Her name it sounds so well,
With sparkling eyes and looks so neat

# Epha Belle

### 3

This modest fair one goes to school,
To learn to read and spell;
And when the teacher calls her out,
She answers Epha Belle.

### 4

A pretty name, it charms the ear;
Can any guess, or, tell
The full true name of one so fair,
As charming Epha Belle.

### 5

Now all the girls that go to school,
I love them passing well;
Obey your teacher, mind the rule,
Keep pace with Epha Belle.

### 6

And now dear pupils one and all,
Strive always to excel;
Let nothing keep you out of school,
But, come with Epha Belle.

### 7

The girls have all sweet names I know,
But none does this excel;
This handsome name where did you go
To find it Epha Belle?

### 8

Miss Gerrand is your teacher good;
May be she can tell;
And let all know about the one
We call Miss Epha Belle.

### 9

Now all good girls that go to school
Must learn their lessons well;

# Erny There

A blossom sweet, so tender and young;
Only awhile on the breast it hung;
Only awhile was life's short stay,
'Til loves sweet blossom pass'd away.
We mourn for this dear lov'd one gone,
His life cut short in early morn,
But faith in God's inspiring love,
Says, look aloft, the light's above.
In Abram's bosom far away,
Where night is lost in endless day,
Where gems of love bloom ever fair,
Look and behold dear Erny there.

# The Shadow on the Wall

9

Again I tried another plan
  My cause it would advance;
And try to live a better man
  By preaching temperance.
But soon comes up that horror still,
  Like Banquos ghost at call,
And sits reclining there at will,
  A Shadow on the wall.

10

The Dearest treasure here on earth;
  The highest point in fame,
The only one of any worth,
  Is virtues noble name.
My kind young friends let nothing blast,
  Nor heed the Tempters call;
So live that early life will cast
  No shadow on the wall.

                      Wayside

## Gone there

A Blossom sweet, so tender and young,
Only awhile one the breast it hung;
Only awhile was lifes short stay,
Til loves sweet blossom passed away.
We mourn for this dear loved one gone,
His life cut short in early morn,
But faith in Gods inspiring love
Says, look aloft, the lights above.
In Abrams bosom far away,
Where night is lost in Endless day,
Where Gems of love bloom ever fair,
Loved and held dear gone there

# Fire

### 1.

At dead of night while good men slept,
While angels watch'd o'er Neponset;
Arose a dreadful sound, most dire,
Wake up!  Wake up!  Fire!  Fire!
It seemed somewhat like Gabriel's Trump,
For men came running on the jump;
While women gather'd in a huddle,
With wan, pale cheeks and direst trouble.

### 2.

Such hurrying there was to an fro,
Like meteor sparks the fireman go,
Still screamed the engine, louder, higher,
And bellowing answer'd Fire!  Fire!
Like frighten'd sheep the women stand
Like speechless; while the fire grand,
With raging splendour, dread, profound,
Scatter'd destruction all around.

## 3.

But all at once, a scream most wild;
A mother's cry "My child!!  My child!!"
Rang out the sound of wild despair;
"My child, my child, O where, O where!!"
The hero of this trying hour,
Was gazing on King Fires Power;
And heard the mother's piercing cry;
Resolved to save the child, or die.

## 4.

With courage bold, undaunted sway,
He bounded up the smoky way;
While fainting hearts as pierc'd with pain,
The thought he'd ne'er return again,
Few moments then did intervene,
Of dread suspense; but soon was seen,
Brave Olley who with brightest smile,
Says "Praise the Lord I've say'd the child."

                                        Wayside

# Fire

Sam. Ben

## 1

At dead of night while good men
While Angels watch'd o'er Nepon
Arose a dreadful sound, most
Wake up! Wak up! Fire, Fire!
It seemed somewhat like Gabriel Tru
For men came running on the jur
While women gather'd in a huddle,
With wan, pale cheeks and direst tro

## 2

Such hurrying there was to an fire,
Like meteor sparks the fireman go
Still screamed the Engine, louder,
And bellowings answer'd Fire!
Like frighten'd sheep the women
Ran shrieklessly; while the fire
With

Such hurrying there was to engage,
Like meteor sparks the firemen go
Still screamed the engine, louder, higher
And bellowings answer'd Fire! Fire!
Like frighten'd sheep the women stand
All speechless; while the fire so grand,
With raging splendor, dread, profound,
Scatter'd destruction all around.

3

But all at once, a scream most wild;
A Mother's cry "My Child!! My Child!!"
Rang out the sound of wild despair;
"My Child, My Child, O where, O where!!"
The Hero of this trying hour
Was gazing on King Fire's Power;
And heard the mother's piercing cry;
Resolved to save the Child, or die.

4

With courage bold, undaunted sway,
He bounded up the smoky way;
While fainting hearts as pierc'd with pain
The thought he'd ne'er return again.
Few Moments then did intervene,
Of dread suspense; but soon was seen
Brave Olley who with brightest smile
Says "Praise the Lord I've saved the Child."

Fire                    Sam. Bennetts House

1

At dead of night while good men slept
While Angels watch'd o'er Ponset;
Arose a dreadful sound, most d...
Wake up! Wak up! Fire! Fire!
It seemed somewhat like Gabriels Trump,
For men came running on the jump;
While women gather'd in a huddle,
With wan, pale cheeks and direst trouble.

2

Such hurrying there was to and fro,
Like Meteor sparks the fireman go
Still screamed the Engine, louder, Higher
And bellowings answer'd Fire! Fire!
Like frighten'd sheep the women stand
...; while the fire ...stand,
With raging splendor, dread, profound,
Scatter'd destruction all around.

3

But all at once, a scream most wild;
A Mother's cry "My Child!! My Child!!"
Rang out the sound of wild despair;
"My Child, My Child, Oh here, Oh here!!"
The Hero of this trying hour
Was gazing on King Fires Power;
...heard the mother's piercing cry;
Resolved to save the Child, or die

4

With courage bold, undaunted sway;
He bounded up the smoky way;
While fainting hearts as pierc'd with pain,
The thought he'd ne'er return again,
Few Moments then did intervene,
Of dread suspense: but soon was seen

# FREEDOMS STAR

### 1.

My tale begins in dark, dark days,
When treason flourish'd in many ways;
When stout hearts qualid; the weak made dumb,
By advancing foes and Rebel Drum,
Bold luring lights were seen from far,
Sure tokens of impending war;
The bugles blast and southern host;
When traitors cried out all is lost.

### 2.

That was the time that tried men's soul,
When treason ruled, above control;
And many silent tears were shed,
While treason flourish'd over-head.
The Star of Hope shone in the West;
The brightest, bravest, and the best;
It shone so bright that all could see,
The Nations Star of Liberty.

3.

Swift to the Nation's rescue come,
Those Stalwart forms, Brave Freedoms Sons;
'Twas freedoms call, 'Twas freedoms sigh;
And freedom was the battle cry.
From Northern Hills and Rock-bound coast,
And western plains came freedom's host,
They saw that beacon from afar;
The greatest light brave freedom's star.

4.

Loud thunders from the Dogs of War;
Design'd to crush Fair Freedom's power;
Was forc'd to yield in wild despair;
Surrender'd all to Freedoms Star.
This Soldier bold, brave freedom's son,
Whose days grow brighter as they run;
Unborn millions will learn to chant
The honest fame of U.S. Grant.

# Freedoms Star

### 1

My tale begins in dark, dark days,
When treason flourish'd in many ways;
When stout hearts quail'd, the weak made sure
By advancing foes and Rebel Drum.
Bold Luring lights were seen from far,
Sure tokens of impending war;
The Bugles blast and southern host;
When traitors cried out all is lost.

### 2

That was the time that tried men's soul
When treason ruled, above Control;
And many silent tears were shed,
While treason flourish'd over-head.
The Star of Hope Shone in the west;
The brightest, bravest, and the best;
It shone so bright that all could see,
The Nations Star of Liberty.

### 3

Swift to the Nations rescue comes

The brightest, bravest, and the best;
It shone so bright that all could see,
The Nations Star of Liberty.

3

Swift to the Nations rescue comes
Those Stalwart farms, Brave Freedoms
Twas Freedoms call, Twas Freedoms
And Freedom was the Battle Cry.
From Northern Hills and Rock-bound
And western plains came Freedom
They saw That Beacon from afar;
The greatest light Brave Freedoms

4

Loud thunders from the Dogs of Wa
Design'd to crush Fair Freedoms p
Was forc'd to yield — in wild de
Surrender'd all to Freedoms S
This Soldier bold, Brave Free
Whose days grow brighter as th
Unborn Millions will learn t
The Honest Fame of U S S

# Freedoms Star.

### 1

My tale begins in dark, dark days,
When treason flourish'd in many ways;
When stout hearts quaild; the weak made Dumb
By advancing foes and Rebel Drum.
Bold Luring lights were seen from far,
Sure tokens of impending war;
The Bugles blast and Southern host;
When traitors cried out all is lost.

### 2

That was the time that tried mens soul
When treason ruled, above Control;
And many silent tears were shed,
While treason flourish'd over-head.
The Star of Hope Shone in the west;
The brightest, bravest, and the best;
It shone so bright that all could see,
The Nations Star of Liberty.

### 3

Swift to the Nations rescue comes
Those Stalwat forms, Brave Freedoms sons;
Twas Freedoms Call. Twas Freedoms Sigh;
And Freedom was the Battle Cry.
From Northern Hills and Rock-bound coast,
And western plains came Freedoms Host
They saw That Beacon from afar;
The greatest light Brave Freedoms Star.

### 4

Loud thunders from the Dogs of War;
Design'd to crush Fair Freedoms power;
Was forc'd to yield— in wild despair;
Surrender'd all to Freedoms Star.
This Soldier bold, Brave Freedoms son
Whose days grow brighter as they run;

# GAMBOLS ON
# THE GREEN

### 1.

Over the mountains, far away;
Where I was born Ms. Nettie.
Where many boys and girls did stay,
In Darksville - pleasant city.
Mid flow'ry plains and mountain scene,
Near by Potomac's tide;
In Shenandoah's Valley, Green,
Was born your friend Wayside.

### 2.

'Twas thirty miles this valley wide,
Where grand old cedars grew;
And lofty pines that seem'd to hide.
Their top in Ether Blue.
I roam'd this valley far and wide;
I've trod the height sublime;
Above the thunder-cloud did ride,
Where all was bright sunshine.

### 3.

My native home; I love it well;
North Mountain just in view;
The other one across the dell,
The grand old Ridge of Blue.
Just five and forty years since,
My native hills have seen.
And any of her mountains high,
Nor of her valley's green.

### 4.

There often in the shade so cool,
To while away an hour;
Would meet together and play school,
In that delightful bower.
That good old home, so very dear,
By me is no more seen;
Nor any of those boys and girls,
Who gambol'd on the green.

### 5.

Yet mem'ry sweet, a charm it lends,
And brings all back to view;
The valley, green, and mountain, glen,
And ridge forever blue.
There on the commons oft did meet,
The young and sweet sixteen,
With happy smiles each other greet,
And gambol on the green.

## 6.

But one there was, a sister, fair,
Who often there was seen,
With Nellie, who would smiling come,
To gambol on the green.
Full fifty years have pass'd away,
Since sister there was seen;
She died and left there, alone
To gambol on the green.

## 7.

And often on the green sward there
I now remember well;
The bright blue eyes and auburn curls
Of charming little Nell
She too is gone and left the green,
Her home there's none can tell,
Nor what became of that dear one,
My charming little Nell.

## 8.

The bright dew-drops of early morn
No longer with me stay;
The smiles of youth -- the tender bloom,
Have faded all away.
Yet ev'ry day the boys and girls
Together there convene,
Joust like the ones who us'd to meet,
And gambol on the green.

## 9.

While down the stream of time we glide
Returns that same old scene;
Of boys and girls playing hide,
And gam'bling on the green.
Where e'er I go wherever roam,
Returns that pleasant scene;
Of child-hoods gay and early bloom,
Those gambols on the green.

## 10.

One little girl I often meet
Then starts the tear unseen;
And moisture fills the eye for one
Who gambled on the green.
My span of life is almost run;
I go to a land unseen
To meet with those that's gone before,
Who gambol'd on the green.

Wayside

Gambols on the Green

1

Over the mountains, far away,
Where lives born boys little;
Where many Boys and Girls did stay
In Darksville—pleasant city.
Mid flowery plains and mountain scenes
Up by Potomac's tide;
In Shenandoah's Valley, Green,
Was born your friend Wayside.

2

'Twas thirty miles this valley wide,
Where grand old cedars grew;
And lofty pines that seemed to hide
Their tops in ether Blue.
Dreamed this valley far and wide;
I've trod the height sublime;
Above the Thunder-cloud did ride,
Where all was bright sunshine.

3

My native Home, I love it well;
North Mountain just in view;
The other one across the dell,
The Grand Old Ridge of Blue.
Just five and forty years since I
Thy native hills have seen.
Not any of her mountains high,
Nor of her valleys green.

4

There often in the shade so cool,
To while away an hour;
Would meet together and play school,
In that delightful bower.
That good old home, so very dear,
By me is no more seen;
Nor any of those Boys and Girls

The Lincoln boys little;
Where many boys and girls did stay
In Parksville—pleasant city;
Mid flowry plains and mountain scene,
Hard by Potomac's tide;
In Shenandoah's Valley, Green,
Was born your friend _____
2
Twas thirty miles this valley wide,
When grand old Cedars grew;
And lofty pines that seem'd to hide
Their tops in ether Blue.
Roam'd this valley far and wide;
I've trod the height sublime;
Above the Thunder-cloud did ride,
Where all was bright sunshine.
3
My native home, I love it well;
North Mountain just in view;
The other one across the dell,
The Grand Old Ridge of Blue.
Just five and forty years since I
My native hills have seen,
And any of her mountains high,
Nor of her valleys green.
4
There often in the shade so cool,
To while away an hour;
Would meet together and play school,
In that delightful bower.
That good old home, so very dear,
By me is no more seen;
Nor any of those boys and girls
Who gambol'd on the green.

Gambels on the Green

5

Yet mem'ry sweet, a charm it lends,
And brings all back to view;
The valley, green, and mountain glen,
And Ridge forever Blue.
There on the Commons oft did meet,
The young and sweet sixteen,
With happy smiles each other greet,
And gambol on the Green.

6

But one there was, a sister, fair,
Who often there was seen
With Allie, who would smiling come
To gambol on the Green.
Full fifty years have passed away,
Since Sister there was seen;
She died and left there, alone
To gambol on the Green.

7

And often on the green sward there
I now remember well,
The Bright Blue eyes and auburn curls
Of charming Little Nell.
She too is gone and left the Green,
Her Home there none can tell,
Nor what became of that Dear One,
My Charming Little Nell.

8

The Bright dew-drops of early morn
No longer with me stay;
The smiles of youth — the third bloom,
Have faded all away;
Yet every day the Boys and Girls
Together there convene
Just like the ones who used to meet,
And gambol on the Green

While down the stream of Time we glide
Returns that same old scene;
Of Boys and Girls playing kids,
    And gambling on the Green.
Where ever I go wherever roam,
    Returns that pleasant scene;
Of Childhoods gay and early bloom,
    Those gambols on the Green.

10

One little Girl Igten meet
Then stole the true unseen;
And moisture fills the eye for one
    Who gamboled on the Green.
The span of life is almost run;
    I go to a land unseen
To meet with those that's gone before,
    Who gamboled on the Green.

# Golden Hair

### 1.

The sweetest carol ever sung,
That ever fell from one so young;
Was wafted on the evening air,
From that sweet singer Golden Hair.

### 2.

In rapture there entranced I stood;
Whence came those sounds so sweet and good,
When all at once, a vision rare
Came singing gaily Golden Hair!

### 3.

So fairie like and voice so sweet;
With bright blue eyes and such small feet;
Such rosy cheeks and face so fair,
Cupids beauty Golden Hair.

### 4.

This young fair one so bright and gay,
In sportive song did whirl away;
As floats the sound on evening air
Came back the song of Golden Hair.

## 5.

I feel sweet inspirations lay,
While visions bright around me play;
The soul is fill'd with music rare
As floats the song of Golden Hair.

Wayside

## Golden Hair (Bessie Shoemaker)

The sweetest carol ever sung,
That ever fell upon one so young;
Was wafted on the evening air,
From that sweet singer Golden Hair.

2
In rapture there entranced I stood;
Whence came those sounds so sweet and good,
When all at once, a vision rare
Came singing gaily Golden Hair!

3
So fairie like and voice so sweet;
With bright blue eyes and such small feet,
Such rosy cheeks and face so fair,
Cupid's Beauty Golden Hair.

4
This young fair one so bright and gay,
In sportive song did whirl away;
As floats the sound on evening air
Came back the song of Golden Hair.

5
I feel sweet inspiration's Lay,
While visions bright around me play;
The soul is filled with music rare
As floats the song of Golden Hair.

Wayside

# INDEPENDENCE DAY

## 1.

A glorious day is now upon us,
The standard theme is freedom's chorus,
That proud old banner waves before us,
The symbol of the free.
Baptized in blood on Bunker-Hill,
Where freedom's sons their blood did spill,
Which fired all hearts with courage, will,
To strike for liberty.

## 2.

For seven long years a stormy blast,
O'er all the skies a lowering cast,
A tyrant power with armies vast,
Defied Columbia's powers.
Brave freedom's sons with courage rare,
On bended knees did bravely swear,
For freedom's rights to do, and dare;
For this fair land of yours.

3.

Those dark, dark days have passed away,
Columbia's sons do now bear sway,
With songs of triumph hail the day,
This independence morn,
When freedom's sons first saw the light,
It shone all with a lustre bright,
Made tyrants tremble with affright,
When this nation, it was born.

4.

Awake!  And sing dear freedom's song;
Awake!  And swell the joyful throng;
Awake!  The echo and prolong,
The nation's jubilee.
Awake!  In rapture freedom's choir,
Awake, and pitch the chorus higher,
Awake the soul's sincere desire,
The love of liberty.

5.

Let bonfires blaze on ev'ry hill;
With anthems sweet and music's thrill;
Make echo's bound from hill to hill;
And bear the news away.
Bid lightning's flash and thunders roll;
And bear the news from pole to pole;
That we are one a perfect whole,
On Independence Day.

## 6.

Fair freedom's daughters wake the strain,
With music fill Columbia's plain;
And sing those battles o'er again,
In rapid round e lay.
A welcome song, arise and sing;
In concert let your voices ring;
Proclaim to all we have no king;
'Tis Independence Day.

## 7.

O, pleasing thought, inspiring strain;
This is the day of freedom's reign;
No tyrant-King, shall ever stain,
Fair Columbia's shore.
The temple, freedom, here shall stand,
A monument, both great and grand;
A bulwark to Columbia's land,
'Till time shall be no more.

## 8.

Unfurl the banner, let it wave
In honor of the gallant brave;
Who ventur'd all this land to save
In that dark trying hour,
Long did the raging conflict last;
Gainst leaden hail, and flurry's blast,
And conquer'd all this Army vast.
The tyrant's dreadful power.

Poetry By Wayside
Book One Freedoms Star
By Wayside


9.

Now raise voices to the skies;
In holy rapture let them rise;
Give God the praise for this dear prize;
To Him our homage pay.
This glorious day has given birth,
The richest boon to man on earth,
More than all tyrants, Kings, are worth,
This Independence Day.

10.

Come, Hark!  The echo long and loud;
Rejoice!  Rejoice!  Still cries the crowd;
The storm of war, the angry cloud
Have all pass'd away.
The war is past, our trials o'er;
And peace and plenty crowd the shore;
Give God the praise forever-more;
'Tis Independence Day.

11.

These Hireling soldiers, sank from sight;
Their sun went down in darkest night;
Surrender'd all to freedom's right;
And left Columbia's shore.
Come fathers, mothers, children, all
Who live upon this earthly ball;
Come here this day, the Lord extol,
And praise him evermore.

## 12.

O praise the Lord both young and old;
We are not slaves that's bought and sold;
But freedom's sons that's true and bold;
Who none but God obey.
Come, fling your banner to the breeze;
And let it wave from all the trees,
Let all discard and jarring cease,
On Independence Day.

97

## Independence Day

1

A glorious Day is now upon us,
The Standard theme is Freedoms Chorus,
That proud old banner waves before us,
   The Symbol of the Free.
Baptized in blood on Bunker Hill,
Where Freedoms sons their blood did spill,
Which fired all hearts with courage, will,
   To strike for liberty.

2

For seven long years a stormy blast,
O'er all the skies a lowering cast,
A tyrant power with armies vast,
   Defied Columbia's power.
Brave Freedoms sons with courage rare,
On bended knees did bravely swear,
For Freedoms rights to do, and dare,
   For this fair land of ours.

3

Those dark, dark days have passed away,
Columbia's sons do now bear sway,
With songs of triumph hail the day,
   This Independence morn.
When Freedoms sons first saw the light,
It shone all with a lustre bright
Made tyrants tremble with affright,
   When this nation, It was born.

4

Awake, and sing dear freedoms song
Awake, and swell the joyful throng
Awake the echo and prolong
   The nations jubilee.
Hark! in rapture Freedoms choir,

## Independence Day

### 5

Let bonfires blaze on every hill;
With anthems sweet and music's thrill;
Make echoes bound from hill to hill;
And bear the news away.
Bid lightnings flash and thunders roll;
And bear the news from pole to pole;
That we are one a perfect whole,
On Independence Day.

### 6

Fair Freedom's Daughters wake the strain,
With music fill Columbia's plain;
And sing those battles o'er again
In rapid roundelay,
A welcome song, arise and sing;
In concert let your voices ring;
Proclaim to all we have no king;
'Tis Independence Day.

### 7

O, pleasing thought, inspiring strain;
This is the day of freedom's reign;
No tyrant King, shall ever stain,
Fair Columbia's Shore.
The Temple, Freedom, here shall stand,
A monument, both great and grand;
A bulwark to Columbia's land,
Till time shall be no more.

### 8          Second part

Unfurl the Banner, let it wave
In honor of the gallant brave;
Who ventured all this land to save
In that dark trying hour,
Long did the raging conflict last,
Quickly flew their shot, and loud their blast

101

## Independence Day

9
Now raise voices to the skies;
In holy rapture let them rise;
Give God the praise for this surprise,
To Him our homage pay.
This glorious Day has given birth,
The richest boon to man on earth,
More than all tyrants, Kings, are worth,
This Independence Day.

10
Come, Hark! the echo long and loud;
Rejoice! Rejoice! still cries the crowd;
The Storm of war, the angry cloud
Have all burst away.
The war is past our trials o'er,
And peace and plenty crowd the shore;
Give God the praise forever more;
Its Independence Day.

11
These Hireling soldiers sank from sight;
Their Sun went down in darkest night;
Surrendered all to Freedoms right
And left Columbias shore.
Come fathers, mothers, Children, all
Who live upon this earthly Ball;
Come here this day, the Lord extol,
And praise him evermore.

12
O praise the Lord both young and old;
We are not slaves thats bought and sold;
But Freedom's sons thats true and bold
Who none but God Obey.
Come, fling your Banner to the breeze;
And let it wave upon the trees;

# Run The Machine

Oh who will unfold in poetic style,
Uncover the errors of things that are vile?
Then open the veil that hides the unseen,
And learn the best way to run The Machine.

And must have disturb the powers that be,
For who can explain the great mystery,
Can we gather light that's from the farthest shore,
And learn how they run things there ever more.

Oh who will unfold in, dramatic style
...
show open the veil that hides the unseen
and learn the best way to run the machine

and ... disturb the powers that be
...
Can we get ... that ... the farther shore
and learn how they run things there ...

# THE BLEEDING HEART

### 1.

Unnumbered blessings round me roll,
Which soothe and warm the dying soul;
But thoughts of others days upstart,
And ope afresh the "Bleeding Heart."
The fancied bliss of days gone by,
In blasted heaps around me lie;
Ingratitude's base, poison'd dart,
Has pierced again the Bleeding Heart.

### 2.

With all my hopes and prospects blasted;
And all the misery I've tasted;
Can love's sweet dream to me impart,
New life to this, my Bleeding Heart!
My days draw near the setting sun;
My race for life is almost run;
Will God new life to me impart,
Revivify and change the heart?

3.


In sorrow deep -- with anguish bent,
Must travel alone the steep descent;
Where sun and moon doth no more shine
To soothe this broken heart of mine.
And there unconscious ever lie,
'Til God shall call me from on high;
Faith, hope, and love to me impart,

4.


When time is o'er with me at last,
When through the gates of death I've passed
Will my poor soul then upward soar
Where bleeding hearts are known no more
With soul renew'd, my troubles o'er,
Can rest in peace forever-more
Where God's free grace new life imparts
New life to this, my bleeding heart.

# The Bleeding Heart

**1**

Unnumber'd blessings round me roll,
Which soothe and warm the dying soul;
But thoughts of other days up start,
And ope afresh the "Bleeding Heart"
The fancied bliss of days gone by,
In haste I heap around me lie;
Ingratitude's base, poison'd dart
Has pierced again the Bleeding Heart.

**2**

With all my hopes and prospects blasted;
And all the misery I've tasted;
Can love's sweet dream to me impart,
New life to thee, My Bleeding Heart?
My days draw near the setting sun,
My race for life is almost run;
Will God new life to me impart,
Revivify and change the Heart?

**3**

In sorrow deep, with anguish bent,
Must travel along the steep descent;
Where Sun and Moon doth no more shine,
To soothe this Broken Heart of mine,
And those unconscious are lie,
Til God shall call me from on High;
Faith, Hope, and Love to me impart,
And heal this Broken Bleeding Heart.

**4**

When time is over with me at last,
When through the Gates of Death I've pass'd
Will my poor soul then upward soar
Where Bleeding Hearts are known no more
With soul renew'd, my troubles over,
Can rest in peace for ever more
Where God's free Grace new life imparts

## The Bleeding Heart

Unnumber'd blessings round me roll,
Which soothe and warm the dying soul;
But thoughts of other days, up start,
And ope afresh the "Bleeding Heart"
The fancied bliss of days gone by,
In blasted heaps around me lie;
Ingratitude's base, poison'd dart,
Has pierced again the Bleeding Heart.

With all my hopes and prospects blasted,
And all the misery I've tasted;
Can love's sweet stream to me impart,
New life to this, My Bleeding Heart?
My days draw near the setting sun,
My race for life is almost run;
Will God new life to me impart,
Revivify and change the Heart?

3

I answered .......................
Must travel alone the steep descent;
Where Sun and Moon doth no more shine
To soothe this Broken Heart of mine
And there unconscious ever lie,
Til God shall call me from on High;
Faith, Hope, and Love to me impart,
And heal this Broken Bleeding Heart.

4

When time is over with me at last,
When through the Gates of Death I've passed
Will my poor soul then upward soar
Where Bleeding Hearts are known no more
With soul renew'd my troubles o'er,

# THE DEACONS CHARGE

## A BURLESQUE

### 1.

Hark!  how the rolling tide,
Deep sounding far and wide,
From hill and mountain side
    Rolls the "Six hundred,"
Quickly the sword unsheathe,
Quickly with bated breath,
Right into the jaws of death,
Dashed the Six hundred.

### 2.

No mortal tongue can tell
How nobly they fought and well,
Fought til the deacon fell,
But never surrendered;
What dreadful thundering?
Soon they fell floundering,
All of them wondering,
Who it was blundered.

### 3.

Backward they turned again,
Back from the slaughter-pen
All of those valiant men,
     Those six-- (hundred)
All that was left of them
Brave and true hearted men
Out of deaths slaughter pen
     Only six-- (hundred).

### 4.

Men of worth brave and bold
Men that can't be bought and sold
Men unspotted pure as gold
     Six--(hundred).
All so holy fair and bright
Which glisten in the morning light
All their plumes so dazzling white
And all of them numbered.

### 5.

A stalwart made to love and bless,
To curl his mustache and caress
Be ready for a smiling kiss
     and then not tarry
Smile and bless my lucky train
And live my life once o'er again
And learn the truth, learn it plain
     and then to marry.

Wayside

183

The Deacons Charge or ~~continued~~ Balaklava
revised  (A Burlesque)

1
Hark! how the rolling tide,
Deep sounding far and wide,
From hill and mountain side
    Rolls the "Six hundred,"
Quickly the sword unsheath,
Quickly with bated breath,
Right into the jaws of Death,
    Dashed the Six hundred.

2
No mortal tongue can tell
How nobly they fought and well,
Fought till the Deacon fell,
But never surrendered;
What ~~dreadfelt~~ thundering?
Soon they fell floundering,
All of them wondering
    Who it was blundered.

3
Backward they turned again,
Back from the slaughter pen
All of those valiant men,
    Those six (hundred)
All that was left of them
    Brave and true hearted men
Out of Deaths slaughter pen
    Only six — (hundred)

4
Men of worth brave and bold,
Men that cant be bought and sold,
Men unspotted pure as gold
    Six — (hundred)
All so poly fair, and bright
Which glisten in the morning light
And their plumes so dazzling white
    and all of them numbered.

A stalwart braide to live and bless,
To curl his mustache and caress
Be ready for a smile or kiss
And there not tarry
So smile and bless my lucky train
And live here life once over again
And learn the truth, learn it plain
And then to (Morris)

Wayside

# The Soldier's Grave

## Decoration Day

### 1.

Cover them over yea gentle fair,
Flowers deck the soldier's bier
For freedom's right their life they gave,
And now they fill a soldier's grave.

### 2.

We feel the awe-inspiring scene,
While looking o'er those hillocks green,
The humble home, the lonely bed,
Where now repose the gallant dead.

### 3.

When love sends forth its brightest ray,
It gilds life's close eventful day;
It stirs the heart and bosoms swell;
When thinking of the ones who fell.

## 4.

Let tender hands the bouquet's spread
Where now repose the patriot dead,
Bid Heaven's rain and gentle showers,
Revive and keep alive those flowers.

## 5.

In humble mood uncovered stand,
And honors give to freedom's band;
Then mingle here your tears with ours,
While we deck their graves with flowers.

## 6.

Yes, cover the couch with roses fair,
With odors sweet, come fill the air,
Bid Heaven smile and earth to bloom,
While we deck the soldier's tomb.

## 7.

When standing at the soldier's bier,
Love's sweet smile will shed a tear,
Then fill the couch with bouquets sweet,
With flowers crown the winding sheet.

## 8.

The spirit, soul, has fled away,
And left behind its kindred clay,
Then kneel and bless those friends of ours,
While we deck their graves with flowers.

9.

Let gentle hands the mantle spread,
With flowers crown the living dead,
The tears may flow and silent creep,
Nought will disturb the soldier's sleep.

10.

Their day is past, their trials o'er
They're anchored on the other shore,
Are waiting now for friends to come,
And share with them "The Harvest Home."

11.

We here behold the fair one's tread;
The silent walk among the dead,
Shed tears of grace than loving roam,
With flowers deck the silent home.

12.

The kind return that greets me here,
Touches the heart, the tender tear,
With chords of love bonds friendship's hand,
Cemented by the strongest hands.

13.

Ye loving fair ones hearts so true,
I thank you for the boys in blue,
I thank you for the flowers given,
The soldiers foretaste here of Heaven.

### 14.

You have our thanks while life shall last,
And when the mystic gates you've passed,
We'll greet you on the shining shore,
And thank you all forever-more.

### 15.

'Tis hope the anchor of the soul,
Revives the heart and keeps us whole,
Tho wild the stormy wind that blows,
Yet life is sweet with all its woes.

### 16.

Then live for life let love make room,
And virtue with your graces bloom;
Then God will bless you every day,
'Till life itself shall wear away.

### 17.

Ye dying souls cover lend your ears,
And catch the music of the spheres
Revolving through the stellar plain,
They tell us we shall meet again.

### 18.

The soldier true with armour bright,
Shall soar above the mystic height to living light,
To that pure zone prepared above,
Where all is life, and all is love.

### 19.

I see the plains and grand review,
Where all appear like "Boys in Blue",
I see the gallant Boys in Blue
I see the hills eternal fair,
Where Boys in Blue dwell ever there,
God and the angels all are there.

### 20.

In silent grandeur let their ashes sleep,
They soon shall mount the upper deep,
In splendour vie the starry plain,
The sleeping soul shall live again.

Wayside

The Soldiers Grave    Decoration Day

while we ..... o'er ..... our ..... duty, then,    and to them ..... day
Who ..... ..... ..... Soldiers bore
For Freedom's right their life they gave,
And now they fill a soldiers grave.

2
We feel the Awe inspiring scene,
While looking o'er these fields green,
The humble home, the lonely Bed,
Where now repose the Gallant Dead.

3
When love sends forth its brightest ray,
It gilds lifes close eventful Day,
It stirs the heart and bosoms swell,
When thinking of the Ones who fell.

4
Let Tender Hands the Bouquets spread
Where now repose the patriot Dead,—
Bid Heavens Rain and gentle showers,
Revive and keep alive those flowers,

5
The humble mound uncovered Stand,
And honors give to Freedoms Band,
Then mingle here your tears with ours,
While we deck their graves with flowers.

6
Go Cover the couch with roses rare,
With odors sweet, come o'er the air,
Bid Heaven Smile and Earth to bloom,
While we deck the Soldiers Tomb.

7
When Standing at the soldiers Bier,
Loves sweet Smile will start a tear,
then Soft fill the couch with Bouquets sweet,
With flowers crown the winding Sheet.

The Soldier's Grave     (Decoration Day) Concluded

The spirit soul has fled away,
And left behind its kindred clay,
Then kneel and bless these friends of yours,
While we deck their graves with flowers.

9
Let gentle hands the wreath spread,
With flowers crown the loving dead,
The tears may flow and silent creep,
Nought will disturb the Soldier's sleep.

10
Their day is past, their trials o'er,
They're anchored on the other shore,
Are waiting now for friends to come,
And share with them the harvest home.

11
We here behold the vacant stead,
The silent walk among the dead,
She'll keep [ ] quiet this loving room,
With flowers to deck the silent tomb.

12
The kind return that greets me here,
Touches the heart, the tender tear,
With words of love binds friendship's bond,
Cemented by the strongest bonds.

13
Ye loving dear ones hearts so true,
I thank you for the Boys in Blue,
I thank you for the flowers given,
The Soldier's foretaste now of Heaven.

14
You have our thanks while life shall last,
And when the music gates you've passed,
We'll greet you on the shining shore,
And thank you all forever more.

The Soldiers Grave Continued

15
'Tis Hope the Anchor of the soul
Revives the heart and keeps us up...
... with the stormy wind that ...
Yet life is sweet with all its woes.

16
Then live for life let love make room,
And virtue with your graces bloom;
Even God will Bless you every day,
Till Life itself shall wear away.

Ye dying souls ... lend your ear,
... catch the ... of the ...
Resolving through the ... there,
They tell us we shall meet again.

18
The soldier true ...
Shall ...
To that ... gone prepared above,
Where all is life, and all is love.

19
See the Plain ... Grand review
Where all appear like "Beings blue"
See the Hills Eternal Fair
Where ...

20
In Silent Grandeur ... them sleep
They ... shall mount the ... steep
In Splendor die the starry plain,
The Soldier true Shall live again.
Sleeping soul

# YELLOW JACK

## IN MEMPHIS 1878

### 1.

I've wander'd away from my own native home;
In quest of the beautiful I did roam;
An anthem sweet from every mouth,
A beautiful song, "The Sunny South."
I turn'd my back to my native hills,
And bracing air which always thrills,
The blood with its wholesome breath;
And found myself in this land of death.

O carry me back to my native home,
And there will I stay and never roam;
O!  Carry me home!  O carry me back!
Away from the land of Yellow Jack!!

## 2.

O take me away to my native hearth,
To that good mother that gave me birth,
Away from fever and deadly chills.
Away to my home and native hills.
The Sirens Song allur'd me away,
To this land of death and misery.
My calls unheeded 'tis most unkind,
No help from any for all seem blind.

> O carry me back to good old mother,
> To father and sister and loving brother;
> O carry home, O, carry me back,
> Away from this monster Yellow Jack.

## 3.

The young and the old, the gay and the proud;
The feeble and strong, all heads are bow'd;
Old Leviathan plunges along,
And scatters dismay in every throng.
Awail of despair from ev'ry mouth;
And groans of the dying fill the South.
The vomit!  The yellow fever is here!
The dead and dying everywhere!

> O carry me back to my good old home!!
> Never-more will from it roam!!
> O, carry me home, O, carry me back!!
> Away, away from Yellow Jack!!

4.

Those poisoned zephyrs softly creep,
And seal their victim while asleep;
Steals in at the door, or, window open,
And leaves death's mark as a sign or token.
From waters that flow through dismal shades;
From swamps and bogs of the Everglades;
The heavens are fill'd with a poison'd air;
Death and destruction all everywhere.

O, carry me back to my home once more;
To my native hills and northern shore;
O, take me away, O, carry me back!!
Away from this monster Yellow-Jack!!

5.

My heart is wrung with a constant care;
With ceaseless watchings and black despair;
That dreadful scourge "Old Yellow Jack,"
Moves a deeper swatch and a wider track.
O, bear me away from this Southern land;
To my good old home on the mountains grand;
Where sparkling frosts and the fires glow,
To my home on the hills, let me go, let me go!!

O, carry me back to my native hills,
Where nought is known of the sinking chills,
O, carry me home O, carry me back,
Away!  Away from Yellow-Jack!!

## 6.

My pathway's hedg'd on every side;
With dire destruction, far and wide;
The bogs and fens the air both fill
With poison that is sure to kill.
O, take me away from this fever-land,
To my mountain home on the hills to stand;
O home, sweet home with its good pure air,
And old Yellow Jack never comes there.

> O, carry me back to my native hills!
> The very thought my soul it thrills!
> O, carry me home, O, carry me back,
> Away from the scourge of Yellow Jack.

## 7.

Death comes in at every door,
Shows no respect to rich or poor;
In a voiceless grip he holds them all,
And shades his malice with a pall.
When darkness shades the misty deep;
And onward swift its waters sweep;
The sounding whistle is heard no more,
Nor welcomes greet the desert shore.

> O, carry me back to my northern home!
> High on its mountains let me roam!
> O help me from this monster fly!
> Let me go home and there to die!!

8.

No crowded ways along the street;
No loving smile no friends to greet;
No voice is heard, no gentle cry;
Except 'tis those who groan and die.
All is still as darkest night,
All have passed away in fright,
All is silent -- all is is hush'd,
Life and light and being crush'd.

    O, carry me back to my native heath;
    Where life is blessed with pure sweet breath;
    O, carry home, O, take me back!
    O take me away from Yellow Jack!

# Yellow Jack

in Memphis 1878

I've wander'd away from my own Native Home;
In quest of the beautiful I did roam;
An Anthem sweet from every mouth
A beautiful song", The Sunny South.
I turn'd my back to my native Hills,
And bracing air which always thrills
The blood with its wholesome breath;
And found myself in this land of Death.

    O carry me back to my native Home;
    And there will I Stay and never roam;
    O carry me Home! O carry me back!
    Away from the Land of Yellow Jack!!

2

O take me away to my native hearth
To that good mother that gave me birth
Away from fever and deadly chills.
Away to my home and native Hills.
The Syrens Song allur'd me away,
To this land of Death and Misery.
My Calls unheeded tis most unkind
No help from any for all seem blind,

    O carry me back to good old Mother,
    To Father and Sister and loving brother;
    O carry home, O, carry me back
    Away from this monster Yellow Jack

3

The young and the Old, the gay and the proud,
The feeble and strong, all heads are bow'd;
Old Leviathan plunges along,
And scatters dismay in every throng.
A wail of despair from ev'ry mouth,
And groans of the dying fill the South.
The Vomit! the Yellow lives is here!

I've wander'd away from my own Native Home;
In quest of the beautiful I did roam;
An Anthem sweet from every mouth
A beautiful song", The Sunny South.
I turn'd my back to my native Hills,
And bracing air which always thrills
The blood with its wholesome breath;
And found myself in this land of Death.
 O carry me back to my native Home;
 And there will I stay and never roam;
 O carry me Home! O carry me back!
 Away from the Land of Yellow Jack!!

2

O take me away to my native hearth
To that good mother that gave me birth
Away from fever and deadly chills.
Away to my home and native Hills.
The Sirens Song allur'd me away,
To this land of Death and misery.
My Calls unheeded tis most unkind
No help from any for all seem blind
 O carry me back to good old mother,
 To Father and Sister and loving brother;
 O carry home, O, carry me back
 Away from this monster Yellow Jack

3

The young and the Old, the gay and the proud,
The feeble and strong, all hearts are bow'd;
Old Leviathan plunges along,
And scatters dismay in every throng.
A wail of despair from ev'ry mouth,
And groans of the dying fill the South.
The Vomit! the Yellow fever is here!
The Dead and Dying every where!

O, take me away from this fever land,
To my Mountain Home on the hills to stand;
O Home sweet Home with its good pure air,
And old Yellow Jack never comes there.

    O, carry me back to my native Hills!
    The very thought my soul it thrills!
    O, carry me home, O, carry me back,
    Away from the scourg of yellow Jack.

7

Death comes in at every door,
Shows no respect to rich or poor;
In a voiceless grip he holds them all,
And shades his malice with a pall.
When darkness shades the misty deep;
And onward swift its waters sweep;
The sounding whistle is heard no more
Nor welcomes greet the desert shore.

    O, carry me back to my northern home!
    High on its mountains let me roam!
    O help me from this monster fly!
    Let me go home and there to die!!

8

No crowded ways along the street;
No loving smile no friends to greet;
No voice is heard no gentle cry;
Except tis those who groan and die.
All is still as darkest night
All have passed away in fright.
All is silent— All is hush, d,
Life and light and being crush'd.

    O, carry me back to my native heath;
    Where life is blessed with the pure sweet breath;
    O, carry home, O, take me back!
    O take me away from Yellow Jack!

O, take me away from this fever-land,
To my mountain Home on the hills to stand;
O Home sweet Home with its good pure air,
And Old Yellow Jack never comes there.
    O, carry me back to my native Hills!
    The very thought my soul it thrills!
    O, carry me home, O, carry me back,
    Away from the scourge of yellow jack.

### 7

Death comes in at every door,
Shows no respect to rich or poor;
In a voiceless grip he holds them all,
And shades his malice with a pall.
When darkness shades the misty deep;
And onward swift its waters sweep;
The sounding whistle is heard no more
Nor welcomes greet the desert shore.
    O, carry me back to my northern home!
    High on its mountains let me roam!
    O help me from this monster fly!
    Let me go home and there to die!!

### 8

No crowded ways along the street;
No loving smile no friends to greet;
No voice is heard no gentle cry;
Except tis those who groan and die.
All is still as darkest night
All have passed away in fright.
All is silent — All is hush'd,
Life and light and being crush'd.
    O, carry me back to my native heath;
    Where life is blessed with the pure sweet breath;
    O, carry home, O, take me back!
    O take me away from Yellow Jack!

## Yellow Jack — Continued

O, take me away from this fever-land,
To my mountain Home on the hills to stand;
O Home Sweet Home with its good pure air,
And Old Yellow Jack never comes there.

   O, carry me back to my native Hills!
   The very thought my soul it thrills!
   O, carry me home, O, carry me back,
   Away from the scourge of Yellow Jack.

### 7

Death comes in at every door,
Shows no respect to rich or poor;
In a voiceless grip he holds them all,
And shades his malice with a pall.
When darkness shades the misty deep;
And onward swift its waters sweep,
The sounding whistle is heard no more
Nor welcomes greet the desert Shore.

   O, carry me back to my northern home!
   High on its mountains let me roam!
   O help me from this monster fly!
   Let me go home, and there to die!!

### 8

No crowded ways along the Street;
No loving smile no friends to greet;
No voice is heard no gentle cry;
Except tis those who groan and Die.
All is still as darkest night
All have passed away in fright.
All is silent— All is hush,d;
Life and light and being crush'd.

   O, carry me back to my native heath;
   Where life is blessed with pure sweet breath,
   O, carry home, O, take me back!

Poetry By Wayside
Book One Freedoms Star
By Wayside

# THE END

www.ingramcontent.com/pod-product-compliance
Lightning Source LLC
Chambersburg PA
CBHW070104070426
42448CB00038B/1602